Thank you for
Coming on my
Journey!

Brett H. Weiss

Just Give Them a Hug ... and the Rest Will Be Easy

How One Person Can Make the World a Better Place, One Child at a Time

BRETT H. WEISS

Fifty percent of the proceeds of this book will go directly to the Bernard and Elsie Weiss Dago Scholarship Fund.

JUST GIVE THEM A HUG ... AND THE REST WILL BE EASY
How One Person Can Make the World a Better Place, One Child at a Time

iUniverse books may be ordered through booksellers or by contacting:

iUniverse
1663 Liberty Drive
Bloomington, IN 47403
www.iuniverse.com
1-800-Authors (1-800-288-4677)

ISBN: 978-1-5320-1963-0 (sc)
ISBN: 978-1-5320-1961-6 (hc)
ISBN: 978-1-5320-1962-3 (e)

Library of Congress Control Number: 2017904192

Print information available on the last page.

iUniverse rev. date: 05/10/2017

Contents

Preface xi

Foreword.. xiii

Acknowledgments xvii

About the Author.. xix

Kiswahili Glossary.. xxi

Introduction 1

2009 Kenya Trip 7

How the Scholarship Fund Got Started 67

Kenya 2011 Trip..78

Kenya 2013 Trip... 111

2015 Kenya Trip.. 149

Pictures 171

Application Essays 183

Report Cards 187

Student Letters 191

HIV/AIDS Posters from Kenyan Schools.................. 195

Roy Is Going to a University 198

Stories 203

Some Thoughts on Fundraising............................... 217

Personal Reflections...222

Conclusion 227

Quotes about the Book and the Scholarship Fund

Reading *Just Give Them a Hug ... and the Rest Will Be Easy* was as if I had arrived in Dago and met the hardworking, sincere people who have become part of Brett Weiss's life now. His personal journals draw you into a world so different from ours it is almost unimaginable, except that Weiss's words share the emotions, the struggles, and the positive outlook of these people so vividly that you are drawn to become part of a solution to provide education to their young students. With his scholarship fund, Weiss has created a path to do that, albeit in one small way. High praise for the work Weiss is doing and for his commitment to education as a way to improve the quality of life in one small community on the other side of the world.

Jill Holopigian-Rodriquez, retired director,
Bensenville Community Public Library

I have known Brett Weiss and his work with children for many years and cannot imagine a more worthwhile scholarship or group of children than these children in Dago, Kenya. I have chosen to contribute to the Dago Fund over the years for many reasons. One is I admire Brett and the hard work he has put into this endeavor, but I have also seen the results when students from Dago come to the United States to visit. These are bright children eager to learn, grow, and improve their lives—all they need is a chance. Brett's scholarship gives them that chance, and from what I have seen, these kids appreciate everything that is given them and excel in their schooling. Here in the United States, we often take for granted the opportunity to get an education. These children do not—their eagerness to learn, their desire to improve their lives, and their success are why I continue to donate, and plan to for years to come.

Jeri Rogowski, Bartlett High School parent
and fund supporter

Brett Weiss's book takes an extremely in-depth look at his journey through Dago, Kenya; the various initiatives his foundation started; and the many adverse situations he went through to fulfill his passion of teaching and creating a better community. The story takes you through Brett's life in Kenya and makes you feel right in the middle of all the touching moments he faced. Having had Brett Weiss as a teacher in high school, I knew his passion for the Bernard and Elsie Weiss Dago Scholarship Fund, but experiencing it through his writing puts this all in a refreshing and inspirational perspective. I commend everything that Brett Weiss has done so far and hope everyone can experience the stories he has told in this book.

Nishu Shah, former student of Brett Weiss,
current student at the University of Michigan

Once you start this book, you won't be able to put it down, and perhaps it will inspire you to join Brett in supporting children who desperately want to attend school. If you contribute to the scholarship fund, you are part of a team that gives children a path out of poverty.

Shana Greene, executive director,
Village Volunteers

I donate to the Bernard and Elsie Weiss Dago Scholarship Fund not only because every child deserves a chance to get an education but also because I believe and hope that the children given the education will become active in the Dago community and help in all ways possible to improve the quality of life.

Tom Boesch, Bartlett High School parent
and fund supporter

To my parents, Bernard and Elsie Weiss,
who gave me everything I have

To my parents, Bernard and Elsie Weiss,
who gave me everything I have

Preface

Jambo ("Hello" in Kiswahili).

I'm writing this book to share the story of my journey with the remarkable people of Dago, Kenya, who have changed and improved my life in so many ways. Their approach to life can teach all of us in the developed world very valuable lessons. In sharing this journey, I hope that you can help me educate additional Dago children, and I also hope to inspire you to take a journey similar to the one I embarked on, in a poor village of your choice. All children deserve the opportunity to get a great education so they can have real *hope* for lives that give them a serious chance to accomplish their dreams. Let's make the world a better place, one child at a time. Please come with me on this journey.

The cover of the book shows me standing with two of the Dago students. These children and their community have inspired me in ways beyond any words I could choose. There is nothing magical about what I did; you can do it too. Could you be the next person in a picture such as this? Yes you could! Who will the blessed children be?

I will begin each chapter with quotes from some of our scholarship recipients about what education means to them, and I will end each chapter with other quotes that have inspired me and that I hope will inspire you too.

In writing this book, I want you, the reader, to feel like you've accompanied me on my journey—not just my journey to Kenya but also my journey to try to help the people of Dago, which eventually led to the start of the scholarship program. I want you to feel as though you were a part of all of this and are still right there with me.

Karibu ("Welcome"),
Brett Weiss

Foreword

By Shana Greene, Founder and Director of Village Volunteers

In 2009, I received an application at Village Volunteers from Brett Weiss, who wanted to volunteer in Kenya. As a high school social studies teacher who taught AP economics, US history, and international relations, Brett had a particular interest in experiencing immersion in a community where he would learn firsthand about some of the difficulties that were the aftermath of colonialism.

Determined to ask questions and listen, he went fully prepared to learn. His first trip was to Dago, a small village in Western Kenya with palpable poverty. As a teacher, his curiosity was riveted on the children and the education system. What he learned would shake his world and open his eyes to the void that was eroding the success of the next generation.

Brett came back to the States quite moved by his experience in Kenya, as he realized that many of the children he met would never be able to get much of an education and therefore not escape abject poverty.

In an ideal world, it would be a universal right of all children to attend school, regardless of their parents' ability to pay for the required tuition and books. Brett would not just visit and forget the faces and discussions he'd had with children.

Per UNESCO, attending high school—where tuition and the indirect costs of school are often twelve to twenty times more than the monthly income of parents—is out of reach for the poorest households. When a child fails to acquire the basic skills needed to function as a productive, responsible member of society, everyone loses. The cost of *not* educating children far outweighs the cost of educating them.

This was the impetus for Brett to start the Bernard and Else Weiss Dago Scholarship Fund, named after his parents. His goal was to sponsor as many young people as he could through high school, and he set out with the passion and sincerity that have made his program so successful.

Brett is a remarkable person and a very special teacher in a Chicago suburb, who without hesitation took on the goal of educating as many students as he could. He will not accept a new child into the scholarship program until he has enough money to take him or her through all four years of high school. He is hands-on and has a relationship with each child sponsored. He is the children's ambassador and their champion, and he updates sponsors with news of their progress and any special awards they achieve.

Once you start this book, you won't be able to put it down, and perhaps it will inspire you to join Brett in supporting children who desperately want to attend school. If you contribute to the scholarship fund, you are part of a team that gives children a path out of poverty.

Shana Greene
Executive Director
Village Volunteers
5100 S. Dawson St., Suite 202
Seattle, WA 98118
206-577-0515

VillageVolunteers.org (12/31/16)
Facebook.com/villagevolunteers
EmpoweringWomenPeriod.org
Facebook.com/empoweringwomenperiod

For anyone who has an interest in volunteering abroad and helping those in our world who are most in need, I highly recommend that you contact Shana and Village Volunteers today. They are involved in many amazing projects that are making the world a much better place by helping those most in need!

Brett Weiss

Acknowledgments

> I will build dispensaries in this community
> so people can get treatment.
> I will build an orphanage for all of the orphans so they
> can get their basic needs of food, shelter, and clothes.
> —Ralph, scholarship recipient

First and foremost, I want to thank my amazing wife, Chris. None of my work in Kenya could have happened without her love, tremendous patience, and support. Chris is the light and spirit behind everything I do. I also thank her for being my first line and toughest editor.

I thank my beautiful and amazing daughter, Amber, who has always inspired me with her passion and enthusiasm for life.

I thank my son, Gabe, who has taught me a lot about patience and kindness; his wonderful wife, Sara; and their son—my grandson and the cutest little boy ever—Collin John Weiss. Their love for each other always inspires me.

I also need to thank my parents, Bernard and Elsie Weiss. These names should be familiar, as I named the scholarship fund after them. They passed away in 2005 and 2006. They grew up very poor in Chicago and were never able to get a college education. My parents always impressed upon my two younger brothers and me the importance of education. While this all started several years after they passed away, I'm certain that somehow they know all about it and are so very happy about what we have accomplished.

I thank my brother and sister-in-law, Bunny and Carol Ann, and their family for all their love and support with Dago, and for always being there for me.

I thank the people who helped edit this book: my wife, Chris; Jill Holopigian; Nishu Shah; and Shana Greene. I am grateful for the quotes I am using from Jill, Nishu, and Shana, as well as from two other people who have been great supporters, Jeri Rogowski and Tom Boesch.

I thank the many, many people who over the last few years have donated their hard-earned money to this cause. The amount of trust they have shown in me and my work is so special and touching. I really do not have words to express how this makes me feel.

I thank Mama Pamela, Duncan, their entire extended family, and all the awesome people of Dago, Kenya, who have been amazing to work with. While my goal is to help them, the reality is they have done much to help me. I so appreciate their hard work and passion for their community and the many things they have done to assist us with our scholarship fund. They have taught me a lot about what is really important in life. None of the great things that have happened with the fund could have happened without the day-to-day work they do in Kenya for the Dago children and me.

Finally, I thank Shana Greene, the founder and director of Village Volunteers, based in Seattle, Washington. Without her support and guidance from the very beginning of the project and through everything I have done, none of it could have happened. Shana and Village Volunteers are beyond amazing. I invite each of you to check out Village Volunteers (VillageVolunteers.org) to see how they can change your life the way they changed mine.

Asante sana!
Brett Weiss

> Appreciation can make a day—even change a life. Your willingness to put it into words is all that is necessary.
> —Margaret Cousins

About the Author

Brett Weiss was born and raised on the southeast side of Chicago in the 1950s and 1960s. He has a bachelor's degree in political science and economics from Northern Illinois University and a master's degree in urban teacher education from Governor's State University. He has been a high school teacher for eighteen years, during two different periods in his life, teaching subjects like AP economics, economics, international relations, US history, and government. He spent five years running a social services agency and more than twenty years in various sales and sales management positions in the software industry.

In 1980 he received the Outstanding Youth Worker Award from DuPage County, Illinois, and he was one of the Illinois Jaycees Ten Outstanding Persons of 1982. Traveling to Africa was something he always wanted to do, and he finally made his first trip to Kenya in 2009; he went again in 2011, 2013, and 2015. In 2015 he received the Coca-Cola Educator of Distinction Award. He studies and teaches about genocide and human rights, and he's also passionate about interfaith education, serving on the board of the Children of Abraham Coalition. In earlier years, he was on the board of the DuPage County Head Start program.

He has resided in Naperville, Illinois, for more than thirty years, and he and his wife, Christine, have been married for more than thirty-five years and have two adult children, Amber and Gabe. Gabe and his wife, Sara, have a son named Collin.

Most of Brett's life has been about helping children—raising his own son and daughter, coaching youth sports for many years, helping disadvantaged children in the Chicago area, and spending years teaching children in the classroom. This book is all about trying to help children who are among the poorest on our planet.

This is his first book, and he hopes you not only enjoy it but also are inspired to take on a similar journey.

Asante sana

Kiswahili Glossary

Kiswahili is the Kenyan version of Swahili. Here are the Kiswahili words used in this book, along with their definitions:

Jambo: Hello.

Karibu: Welcome.

Matatu: Privately owned minibuses—typically large vans—that are generally designed to hold about fourteen people but usually carry well more than twenty as well as several animals, plus lots of luggage, bags of grain, and so on, inside the van and tied to the top and back of the van. They are generally not in the best of condition. Quite often they are decorated with advertisements and many quotes from the Bible.

Muzungu: White man/person/woman.

Asante sana: Thank you very much.

Ugali: Among the most popular Kenyan foods, prepared by boiling water, adding cornmeal, and stirring and turning the mixture until it forms a dense paste. Also known as *sembe*, this hearty dish goes down well with *sukuma wiki* or meat stew.

Chapati: A piece of flat, thin, often unleavened bread. Chapattis trace their origin from Kenya's Indian population. They can be eaten with any kind of stew or as a snack with chai (tea).

Introduction

> My education will be of great benefit to my community
> because I will provide scholarships to other people
> in the future. I will reveal to my community what
> education is and the importance of education.
> —Hillary, one of our scholarship recipients

Over the last few years, many people have been telling me that I really need to write a book about the work I have been doing in Dago, Kenya. I have always wanted to write a book, and I have started many of them that went nowhere. However, the more I thought about writing a book about Dago, the more excited I became. After all, I pretty much had it written, between some journaling I had done, various talks and presentations I had given, the stories I'd told people, and everything else that was in my head. All I needed to do was put it all together in a format people would enjoy reading, and I would have the book! Today I know it is a bit more complicated than that.

What would the purpose of the book be? I could think of several:

1. To share with readers the amazing journey I'd been on with the outstanding people of Dago
2. To share the process I'd gone through, from just starting off wanting to learn about the people of Dago, to deciding that I wanted to help them, to actually helping them in a number of ways

1

3. To share what I'd learned about how we can help the millions and millions of people who live in abject poverty have significantly better lives
4. To share what I'd decided it takes for a small foundation to be successful
5. To share my amazing stories about the bright, hardworking, fabulous children of Dago
6. To encourage people to help us in our efforts to help even more of these children
7. To inspire others to take a journey similar to the one I took

Africa has always been of great interest to me, and so going into this project, I had many questions: How could one continent have so many challenges, and why isn't more being done about them? What is it like to be African? What is it like to live in a mud hut with no electricity or plumbing? How can we fix this problem of systemic poverty? More specifically, what can I, one person here in the United States of America, do about it?

While I love to travel, the thought of living in a village with families surviving on less than two dollars per day was not exactly my idea of a dream excursion. For years I had thought about going to Africa but had never gone beyond the thinking stage. By 2004, I had been away from teaching for twenty-five years; instead I'd been selling software and managing salespeople. But I decided to return to my true passion and first love, the field of education. One extremely enticing reason was so I could have summers free to travel.

So that year, and for the next few years after I returned to teaching, I thought a lot about Africa, but unfortunately I took no action. I always had an excuse—like "My finger is hurting!" I really was avoiding the issue. I spent much of my time creating excuses instead of plans.

In the last half of 2006, I went through a bit of a health scare that demanded immediate attention. For a few years, my doctor had been monitoring a small lump in my throat. Part of the reason he was concerned was that I was one of those children in the 1950s who underwent radiation treatments for recurrent tonsillitis. In those days it was thought that radiation would be a suitable cure; unfortunately, it was not such a good idea. Finally my doctor referred me to a specialist. A biopsy was ordered, and my nerves were on edge. The needle may as well have been straight from a television crime investigation show. Then the day came for me to get my biopsy results. I sat in the doctor's waiting room, shaking a bit and trying to take some deep breaths. The nurse called me back to an examining room, where I awaited the news as I sat restlessly in a chair. When the doctor entered and announced that the results were negative for cancer, I breathed a big sigh of relief—but then I noticed that he was not exactly smiling. He then said that because of my radiation treatments in the 1950s, he felt we should schedule surgery to take out my thyroid, even though it was functioning perfectly. He explained that just because the biopsy did not show cancer, I was not necessarily cancer-free. In fact, he said, the odds were pretty high that I *did* have thyroid cancer.

Thus surgery was scheduled for December 2006. The day of the surgery came, my thyroid came out, and from then on I had to deal with life without a thyroid, taking a pill each day to do what the thyroid normally did. I set an appointment to meet with the doctor in about a week to get the results of the surgery. Once again, my nerves were on edge, and I worked on taking a lot of deep breaths.

So the day came for the appointment, and again I was in the examining room, waiting for the doctor to arrive. After a hello and some pleasantries, he looked at me and said he was not surprised to learn after the surgery that I did in fact have thyroid cancer. I'd heard many, many people over the years talk about that moment when they were told they had "the big C," but I'd never really thought about it happening to me; that's one of those things we think only happens to other people. As I recall, I was pretty calm on the outside but terrified on the inside.

He went on to explain that we caught it at a very early stage, which was a good thing. He said that they were able to get most of the cancer out during the surgery, but it was impossible to get all of it out, so I was going to need to go through a procedure where I would drink a cup of radioactive fluid and then go home for three days and not be near anyone else. I would need to wear latex gloves, use paper plates and cups and plastic cutlery that I had to throw out in separate bag, and so on. No one could be near me, because if they were, they would be exposed to radiation. After three days I could go back to a normal life, but for six months I would need to carry a card explaining the radiation treatment, because if I went through an x-ray machine, such as one at the airport, it would go off. This treatment would get rid of most of the remaining cancer, the doctor said. I did find it strange that in order to cure something I got because of radiation, I needed to drink something radioactive.

The bottom-line diagnosis was that I would probably go on to live a nice, long, healthy life, and when my time came, I would die of something other than thyroid cancer. Needless to say, however, these were days that weighed on me heavily. I thought a lot about my life, what was really important to me, and how I wanted to spend the rest of my days. I took the time to ponder my future. I thought a lot about my wife, my two children, and my other relatives and friends. And I thought a lot about things I had always wanted to do but always came up with excuses not to do. At the top of that list was going to Africa.

I wanted to turn this scare into a positive. At the end of my life, I did not want to look back at a list of things I had wanted to do but didn't because I kept coming up with weak excuses. Was this the time to get serious about Africa?

There is a great quote from the late sportscaster Stuart Scott that seems very appropriate to share now:

> You beat cancer by how you live, why you live,
> and in the manner in which you live.

As I began my planning for Africa, I came to the quick realization that I had no clue where to start. I could not just get on a plane and fly to someplace in Africa, get off the plane, and upon arrival say,

"Okay, the white guy is here to help you! Just tell me what I can do for you!" I needed a better plan.

So I made lists of the questions I had and what I thought I wanted to accomplish. To be frank, neither list was very long; I realized I needed to put a lot more thought into it. I knew that every day my brain would give me new reasons not to go, but I was determined not to let those excuses win. I came to the conclusion that sacrifices might have to be made, but going to Africa was no longer negotiable. At that point I started to get a real sense of clarity. I knew then that I would go to Africa. I just needed to figure out how and get someone to help me.

> Live as if you were to die tomorrow. Learn
> as if you were to live forever.
> —Mahatma Gandhi

First Volunteer Trip to Kenya, Summer 2009

What follows is from the daily personal journal I kept during my first trip to Kenya, in the summer of 2009. Some updates have been made.

> I would like to enjoy the lovely and sweet fruits of education.
> I would like to bring light and hope to our family.
> —Eunice, scholarship recipient

After months and months of preparation, I was ready (ready or not!) for my first trip to Kenya. I wanted to make sure I wrote down all the things that would be happening in my life during this trip. I felt as though I had been preparing for it my entire life.

Monday, July 27, 2009

At 4:45 p.m., the limo picked me up from my home in Naperville, Illinois. By 5:50 p.m. I was sitting at Gate C20 at O'Hare Airport after having gone through security. I've always been someone who likes to get to the airport extra early, but in this case I kind of went overboard: I still had three hours and twenty-five minutes until takeoff. I had seat 31B on United Airlines flight 938, and at 8:55 p.m., the plane left for London. I was nervous, excited, and filled with adrenaline as we took off. After thinking, dreaming, planning, and hoping for a trip to Africa for so many years, I was now on my way. I wondered what I had ahead of me, knowing that each and every minute of it would be a new and unique experience.

Tuesday, July 28, 2009

I arrived at Terminal 1 at London Heathrow at 11:15 a.m. I did a lot of walking, took a bus, and then did a lot more walking to Terminal 4. The terminal was under construction, so it was quite a mess. I ate some lunch at a place called Garfunkel's and then waited. In booking my trip, I tried to save as much money as possible, and I learned that in general, the longer the layover, the cheaper the price. I booked this trip with a nine-hour layover in London. The main thing I learned in doing this is to never again have a nine-hour layover. I walked and walked and tried to get some sleep by lying down on some seats. For me, falling asleep is never an easy thing, so I was not able to get any sleep in the airport. Finally I was back on a plane and headed to the capital of Kenya, Nairobi.

As I was sitting on the plane getting closer to Kenya, I was reading President Obama's book *Dreams from My Father*. A very special moment for me came as the pilot announced we were getting ready to land. I was at the part in the book where Mr. and Mrs. Obama were making their first trip to Kenya after their marriage. Mr. Obama had never been to Kenya before, and he wanted to visit the land of his father and his relatives. (His father had passed away many years earlier.) Just as I was reading about Mr. Obama preparing to land in Nairobi, I was preparing to do the same thing. I felt a certain kinship with Mr. Obama at that moment, and it put into perspective the reality of what I was getting into. I stepped off the plane excited and ready to explore.

Wednesday, July 29, 2009

I arrived in Nairobi at 6:00 a.m. Getting through customs was much easier than I'd anticipated. I was carrying a yellow immunization card listing all the shots I had taken to make the trip, and I naively thought that customs would check it, but that was not the case. I wondered why they didn't, but moved on. I had carried on two bags and checked two suitcases. After an hour of waiting and finding only one of my two checked suitcases, I decided I needed to file a lost luggage report. I was told it would take twenty-four hours to get me my luggage. It was very frustrating not having one of my bags as I began my first trip to Kenya, but I knew I just needed to go with it and make the best of the situation.

The Nairobi airport (Jomo Kenyatta Airport, named after the first president of Kenya) was incredibly crowded and hot, and it was not the cleanest airport I had ever seen. The luggage area was way too small for the amount of people and luggage it had to serve. I felt like I was at the United Nations, as the airport was filled with people from all over the world. When I was in the customs area, I loved seeing all the different kinds of passports, and I was fascinated by the various styles of clothing I saw and the numerous languages I heard. My first trip to a bathroom—or water closet, as they called it, because Kenya was once a British colony—was not pleasant. It was old, small, and dirty. However, I later realized that it was one of the best bathrooms I would see for the next three weeks.

I was scheduled to spend the night at the home of Wendy, who worked with Village Volunteers and took in volunteers like me. She had a few extra bedrooms for that purpose. When my driver came to pick me up, I felt like I was in a movie: he held up a sign with my name on it and waited. I found him and was soon on my way to Wendy's home.

It was a very interesting drive that took about forty-five minutes. Kenyans drive on the left side of the street and the driver sits on the right side of the car—another hangover from the country's colonial days. It was morning, and the drive gave me a chance to see Nairobi starting its day. It is a city of about 3.1 million people.

The roads were in extremely poor condition and pitted with massive potholes. There were no curbs, garbage was strewn everywhere, and crowds of people were walking all over the place on

9

both sides of the road. The road was packed with vehicles, mostly vans and buses. Driving in an actual lane did not seem to be important.

Signs of extreme poverty were everywhere. I saw all kinds of little huts and small, broken-down homes, but most of the buildings were high-rises, with clothes hanging everywhere. They were in very poor condition—cracked, rusted, dirty, and in great need of repair—and reminded me of high-rise projects I'd seen in the United States. There were buildings with various shops, but those looked very old and broken-down too. There were big signs and billboards on both sides of the road, and there was lots of noise: people shouting, cars honking, and music blaring. It was definitely totally different than anything I had ever experienced. I was trying to absorb as much as possible, as this environment was slowly becoming my new reality.

Also, all around the airport were soldiers with AK–47s on their shoulders. My driver told me the increased security was because the president of Kenya was coming to the airport that morning. I later learned that this level of security was pretty normal. It made me feel safe … I think!

We arrived at Wendy's home, where I met Cindy, who lived with Wendy and helped out with volunteers. We had driven through a lot of poverty-ridden areas to get to their subdivision, which in some ways looked like a middle-class neighborhood in the United States. There was clearly much more security; the entire area was enclosed by a tall metal fence, and its one entry gate, which was solid metal, was monitored by a guard. The roads, again, were extremely poor, and I noticed that each home had its own tall metal fence around it with a locked door in the front. All the windows and doors were protected by metal bars. It was clear that security was important and incredibly tight.

Wendy worked her government job during the day (I learned that her work dealt with drug prevention), so it was Cindy's job to take care of things at home—keeping it clean, making meals, and so forth—while Wendy was at work. I was exhausted, as I had not had any sleep for about thirty-six hours, and so after a brief conversation, I took my stuff (minus my missing suitcase) and went upstairs to my bedroom. They had two extra bedrooms in the house for volunteers, each with two bunk beds. I lay down on my bunk and quickly fell asleep.

Upon waking from a three-hour nap, I met a couple from Australia who were leaving Kenya that night, having completed their volunteer work, and a college student named Samantha, who'd just arrived. Samantha was from California and had just finished her freshman year. I took what turned out to be a pretty nice shower; it was not quite like being at home, but it would be the only real shower I would have for almost three weeks. So I'd had my sleep and a shower, and it felt amazing. And, oh yes, I pinched myself and realized I was in Nairobi, Kenya. It was hard to believe, but I had started my journey in Africa.

The home was a typical middle-class Kenyan home. It had electricity and a nice kitchen with a gas stove, a refrigerator, a microwave, and most of the other amenities Americans would expect. However it was all much smaller than a typical American home. The lower level featured a small living room, dining room, and bedroom in addition to the kitchen. The living room had a flat-screen TV and a DVD player. Upstairs was Wendy's bedroom, as well as the two bedrooms I previously mentioned. There was a bathroom both upstairs and downstairs. They were a bit primitive but functioned pretty much the way a bathroom back home would. There was no washing machine or dryer. There were lights in each room, but the amount of light was very limited. I was told that power in Nairobi was unreliable and went off quite often. I was also told there was a serious water shortage, which worried me a bit.

Cindy agreed to walk Samantha and me to some stores that were only a few blocks away. When we walked by a private primary school, I began to get an idea of how poor the conditions were in schools in Kenya. This was in a nicer area of Nairobi, yet the building had broken windows and its concrete walls were cracked. There were lots of children playing outside in their school uniforms, and that's when I learned that all schoolchildren in Kenya wear uniforms. I also learned that school ran pretty much year-round there. As a teacher, I found this very interesting, as I have always thought it's a real waste that in the United States we spend so much money on educational facilities that sit idle for about a fourth of the year.

In walking around, I could tell this was a heavily Christian area, as I passed by many different kinds of churches. In a little grocery store we visited, there were many religious items for sale, often with images of Jesus. Noticing an ATM near the store, I decided to see if my ATM card actually worked so I could get some Kenyan shillings. I inserted my card, and the words on the machine pretty quickly said, "Welcome Brett H. Weiss." Wow! I was excited and impressed.

Also, I'd had a very pleasant surprise when I woke up from my nap earlier that day: my luggage had actually arrived on my fight but was never brought to the baggage claim. By late afternoon, my luggage had arrived. I breathed a sigh of relief.

Thursday, July 30, 2009

I woke up at 4:45 a.m. Kenyan time (which is eight hours ahead of Illinois time), and by 5:30 I had taken a shower and was packed and ready to be picked up at 6:30 to begin the journey to Dago. I was told it would take about one and a half hours to drive to where we would meet Patrick, the volunteer coordinator; then I'd get on a bus for the trip to Dago, which was supposed to take about eight hours with some stops at various locations along the way.

One of the interesting things I'd learned the night before was that most of Nairobi, a city of more than three million people, had no street signs or addresses. Only the downtown area had them. Thus for someone to get to Wendy and Cindy's home, or most places in Nairobi, you either had to know exactly where you were going ahead of time or else had to get directions from someone who did (such as, "Make a left at the Shell gas station, take a right at the blue house," and so on). Mail was delivered through post office boxes.

I slept pretty well, surprisingly. Windows that had bars protecting them were generally left open to let a breeze come through, and you could hear the sound of dogs barking throughout the night. Then as morning approached, the roosters started doing their thing. It seemed as though many people, even in the city, had roosters and chickens, which were a major part of the Kenyan diet. Clearly I was "not in Kansas anymore"!

Speaking of food, dinner the previous night had been excellent. We had noodles, a hamburger mix with various spices, and mixed veggies. There was also a plate of cut-up avocados and mangos. Wendy and Cindy were magnificent and very gracious hosts.

Cindy was up to prepare breakfast for us before we left for Dago. The night before, I'd heard many stories about Dago from some other volunteers before they left for the airport. The stories about the children and adults who worked there made me even more excited about getting there and experiencing Dago for myself.

At 7:45, we arrived at the center of the city and were dropped off at a gas station that also ran a big business taking people to and from various places in vans. The drive ended up taking about fifteen minutes less than I'd been told; then again, we only went about ten miles. The traffic was the worst I had ever experienced, and I grew up in Chicago. The roads were in very poor condition and were filled with cars, buses, and vans. I learned the word *matatu*, which is the Kiswahili word for "bus." The street was very crowded, with very little respect paid to lanes. There were many rotaries or roundabouts, since the roads had been designed by the British when Kenya was a colony.

We waited for Patrick, who showed up at 8:30 a.m. I had already begun to learn about "Kenyan time": however long you think something is going to take, you might as well double it. Patrick went to get some cash and did not come back until 9:50, but then Samantha and I hit the road in a Toyota van with Patrick and our driver. I noticed that the vast majority of vehicles in Kenya were Toyotas, although I saw a variety of other Japanese and European vehicles too. When I asked if there were many US-made vehicles there, Patrick told me that they were very expensive in Kenya and that only some rich people had them. (By the end of the trip I had not seen any US-made cars except for a few old clunkers.)

The sights and sounds of Nairobi in the morning were amazing—and different and nerve-racking for me. There were the sounds of cars and buses driving and honking, lots of loud music, and people talking as they went to work. There was an incredible amount of traffic (until we left Nairobi), with people walking everywhere. Most people couldn't afford a car or even a bus ride, so they walked to work. The distance between walkers and vehicles was very narrow and dangerous. There were no sidewalks, so people were just walking on the edge or sides of the roads. Many people were well dressed, and others were dressed very casually as they headed to work. I could see many influences of the West in their clothing, such as Nike apparel, Levis, and Cubs, Sox, Yankees, and Mets baseball caps. Later I learned that these clothes either came to Kenya as donations from charities or were bought used on the street for a very small amount of money. There were peddlers everywhere, selling about anything you could imagine.

About a year later, Patrick's now-wife, Susan, who is from Evansville, Indiana, told me a story about the first time he came to the United States. She picked him up at O'Hare, and as they were driving out of the airport, he asked her where all the people were. He was expecting to see lots and lots of people walking alongside the road, as I had seen in Kenya. He was astonished to see no one walking. Susan told him that most people in the United States owned a car, and that those who did not took public transportation. This was a real eye-opener for Patrick on his first day in the United States.

The stores we passed on our journey tended to be very colorfully painted, with bright green, yellow, pink, and orange fronts. During the drive, I tried to use my BlackBerry. Voice was working, but the Internet, e-mail, and texts were not. I could not figure out why, so Wendy got on the phone with Sararicom, the local cell phone provider in Kenya. My cell service stayed this way until Thursday of the next week, when all of a sudden my e-mail worked fine, I could get on the Internet, I could receive texts but not send them, and I could see that I had voice mails but could not check them. In my "normal" world, I would have been greatly bothered by all of this, but in Kenya I just knew it was part the journey, and I had to accept whatever happened. Also, some part of me realized that it would not kill me to get away from the world of having access to instant communication each and every second of every day.

When we finally left the center of the city to make our way to Dago, Patrick said it would take about six hours to reach our destination. At 11:00 a.m. we stopped to visit the Chujia Water Filter Company. They made ceramic water filters, and Patrick bought a number of them to bring to Dago. The owner, who was a retired science teacher, gave us a tour of the facility. He'd started this business after he retired, and it was quite impressive what he was doing. I'd begun to understand that the lack of clean water was a major problem in sub-Saharan Africa, so it looked to me like this business would be very successful. He told us that 60 percent of the deaths in villages like Dago were the result of people drinking bad water, and most of them were children, because when children are thirsty, they do not ask if the water is safe—they just drink it.

Back in the van, I asked Patrick why the government did not just build a filtration system in Lake Victoria, which is on the western border of Kenya and not far from Dago. He explained that the government did not have enough money to do it. This was a real eye-opener for me, as I'd grown up on the southeast side of Chicago near Lake Michigan, which thanks to the city's filtration system supplied us with plenty of good water. Easy-to-access, safe, clean water, which we take for granted, was a very difficult issue for people in this part of the world.

We arrived in Dago at about 5:30 pm. It had been a wild ride to say the least. About half the road was not much of a road at all, and what road there was had numerous potholes. At times the road was down to one and a half lanes or even one lane; other times the road was just gravel and dirt. Plus each time we went through a village, and there were many of them, both sides of the road were crowded with people, cows, goats, sheep, chickens, and so forth. In some villages we stopped to pick up or drop off people; some villages we just drove straight through.

A very scary moment came when we approached a village named Kisii. All of a sudden our van was surrounded by a large group of young men. They made us stop, and they started yelling and screaming at us while holding machetes in their hands and pounding and rocking the van. Obviously this was a nerve-racking experience; my mind drifted to my knowledge of the Rwandan genocide, with large groups of young men carrying machetes. Of course, they were yelling in a language I did not understand. I looked at Samantha and she looked at me, not knowing what to think. I had already learned the concept of a Kenyan toll road, where the police would stop you and you had to pay a "toll" in order to move on, but this was different.

After about ten minutes, we were allowed to move on. Catching my breath, I asked Patrick what that was all about. He said that a Kisii matatu driver had been killed in an accident the week before and they wanted all vehicles that passed through the town to give them money to help the family. I hadn't seen anyone give them money, and so I asked him what he told them. He told them that we were just volunteers and not tourists, so there was no money for them. Eventually they accepted this and let us go. The fact is, Samantha and I each had a great deal of money on us, both US and Kenyan, and I was sure both Patrick and our driver had a lot of money too, but we went forward without giving any of it up. So we were shaken, but most important, we were safe.

We moved ahead and had lunch at a covered restaurant. We all washed our hands with soap and water from a big sink in the middle of the room. Patrick helped us order from a very limited menu. I had chicken and what I would learn was a Kenyan staple, *ugali*—corn flour mixed with water to a porridge consistency and then dried to a cake-like texture. Ugali is very heavy and does not have much taste; it is certainly meant to fill up a hungry stomach with some nutrients.

When we arrived in Dago (the last mile was a very bumpy dirt road), we met Patrick's parents, Duncan and Mama Pamela. They were around my age, and through farming they operated a school and orphanage. I then met two other volunteers: Jyoti, an attorney and educator from London, and Stephanie, a social worker from Toronto. After this we were led to our individual rooms in a cement building that looked very new.

After getting settled, we made our way to the orphanage and jointed a party. The facility had come about because of the massive problem of AIDS in this part of the world. Many children had lost one or both of their parents due to the disease, and the orphanage had been built with the help of a Peace Corps volunteer and some money from the Peace Corps. It held thirty-six girls. I met the orphaned girls and many other children from the area, along with their relatives, including some of the moms who volunteered their time to help out. We spent about three hours playing with the girls and watching them sing and dance. I learned that the children loved to have their photos taken; they would yell, "Photo!" because they knew we had cameras with us. When we took a picture, they'd run up to us to see what they looked like. (Mirrors were very rare there.) After some time, I had to say, "No more photos," as it seemed the picture taking would never end. The children were not happy with me, but I needed to move on and get to the helping.

Another word I learned that day was the Kiswahili word *muzungu*. Quite often, groups of kids would see us and yell out, "Muzungu! Muzungu!" over and over. When I first arrived in Dago, lots of children were running up to me, yelling that, so I had to ask what it meant. I was told it meant "white person." Then I understood why they were yelling that. The children just loved playing with us, and it was clear that they thrived on the love and attention. Some of the younger children would want to touch my skin and hair, as it was so different than any skin or hair they had ever seen. This was a bit strange at first, but perfectly understandable.

After the children went to sleep, we went to Duncan and Mama Pamela's house on the property, where we had dinner and laughed a lot. We ended up eating most of our meals in their home. In this room there were three small tables surrounded by a variety of chairs and couches. The meal's several courses were brought out in covered bowls. The food had been heated over a fire in a separate room. We each had our own bowl with a big spoon, and we would take what we wanted and put it in our bowl. Before each meal, Duncan would say a prayer (although on some nights we took turns). Also, one of their daughters would bring out a big plastic bowl in which they would pour some warm water from a pitcher for us to wash our hands. It was a way for everyone to eat with clean hands; however, we all wiped our hands dry with the same towel, so that kind of defeated the purpose. Each meal brought great food, good conversation, and lots of laughs.

Friday, July 31, 2009

I woke up at about 6:00 a.m. feeling pretty well rested. After washing up and brushing my teeth, I changed and walked around the grounds a bit. This was a working farm, with lots of cows, goats, chickens, and roosters. The air was filled with the sounds of livestock. There were a couple of young men walking around, getting their morning chores done—feeding the animals, milking the cows, and tending to the crops. I took a number of pictures that morning of the beautiful scenery—the sunrise, the rolling green hills, and so forth. There was a small mud hut just on the other side of the property, separated from it by a barbed-wire fence. Several children came out of the hut to play. I waved, and they waved back. Then their mom came out and started a small fire to cook breakfast. Later I learned that their dad had died of AIDS and the mom and children were all "sick," which I later learned meant that they had AIDS too.

Being me, I asked a lot of questions during my short time in Kenya. And each of my questions brought about more questions. Some answers were clear, and some I really did not understand. English is Kenyans' third language, but most of the people I met there spoke English pretty well. However, there were differences in the way they used their words, plus they spoke in an accent that was new to me and could be difficult to understand. There were times when it was hard for me to have a conversation with the local people.

Sometimes I was frustrated by my inability to understand them, and I think at times they were frustrated too. When speaking among themselves, they generally spoke their tribal language, Luo, since they were from the Luo tribe, one of forty-two tribes in Kenya. They also used Kiswahili, the Kenyan version of Swahili. I thought a lot about how I really only knew one language while each of them knew three. There was so much I wanted to learn that I could have spent all day, every day, asking questions. Of course, that was not a good idea. I just had to do the best I could each day.

The night before, Duncan had mentioned that they were Seventh-day Adventists. I'd realized they were very religious people earlier that day, when during the entire ride to Dago we listened to gospel music and the preaching of a Kenyan minister. At dinner, Duncan said to me, "I assume you are a Christian?" I explained that I was Jewish and that my wife, Chris, was Catholic. He did not seem to know exactly what to do with that information, but he was very polite and said, "That is nice."

It was already Friday, and since I'd left my house on Monday afternoon, the time had gone by quickly. I still wasn't quite sure exactly what I would be doing there. Today my plan was to check things out, learn as much as I could, and see where I could be the most help. I was anxious to give the school my gifts: crayons, colored and regular pencils, a sharpener, and two children's books. One was about President Barack Obama and his Kenyan roots, and the other was about NFL coach Tony Dungy. President Obama's father was from a village near Dago and had come from the same Luo tribe as the people of Dago. I'd already learned that they took a great deal of pride in the fact that the son of a Luo man was president of the United States.

I went on to have an amazing morning. About 7:30 a.m., I heard children singing, so I walked over to the Dago Primary School, where the sound was coming from. There were about 150 children singing in a room with a cement floor, brick walls, open windows, and a roof made of sheet metal, which they call "iron sheets." The roof had many small holes in it to let light in, since they did not have electricity. I was told the holes were small enough that rain would not come through.

At times the students would do prayer readings from the Bible; one of the older boys would read a passage while another interpreted it for the students. They would do this in both English and Luo. I was sitting in the back of the room, trying to enjoy what was happening and not interfere, when one of the students got up, left the room, and came back with a chair. He placed the chair at the front of the room and motioned for me to come up to the front and sit there. I tried to tell them that I just wanted to sit in the back, but they insisted. When I got up front, they told me that I was a "special visitor" and they wanted me to sit there. I listened to the children sing and pray for several more minutes. They were sensational, singing a variety of songs, including gospel. I learned that this singing and praying went on each Friday morning before the start of school.

When the students stopped singing and started to walk toward the center area of the school, I went over to a building on the school grounds where the teachers had their "office." In this room there were eight teachers for about four hundred students. Each teacher had his or her own desk, and they covered the first through eighth grades— or class one through class eight, as they said (another expression that remained from Kenya's days of being a British colony). The class eight teacher, Henry, was also the assistant headmaster. The other teachers and I did some "teacher talk"; they had a lot of questions for me about teaching methods. I was already thinking about the challenges teachers had in the United States, while in Kenya teachers were working with no electricity or plumbing in dirty and very crowded classrooms that were little more than mud huts, and with serious limitations on things like books, paper, pens, pencils, and chalk. Actually, on that particular day the teachers had no chalk at all. I learned chalk was very expensive and hard to get.

The schools divided their classes based on ability level, not on chronological age. Thus, you had a number of older students in the lower grades and a number of younger students in the higher grades. I told the teachers about the gifts I had brought, and they asked me to go get them. Then I was told that the headmaster wanted to talk to me. His name was Joseph, and he had his own office. He talked to me about the challenges they were facing and the kinds of things they needed. He was very serious and straightforward.

Next they asked me to personally give the oldest fifty students the fifty pencils I had brought. In the courtyard, they lined up the fifty students, and one by one I gave each of them a pencil and shook each child's hand as he or she said thank you. I remember thinking as I did this, *Wow, here I am in a tiny village in Africa, handing pencils to elementary school children*. It was an unreal feeling. Then I pulled out a little plastic sharpener and learned that none of them had ever seen a pencil sharpener before. They sharpened their pencils by whittling them with a knife. One of the teachers mentioned how dangerous it was for the children to whittle; quite often they would cut themselves. In a community where there was little basic medical care, this was a big problem. So I showed them how to use the sharpener, and you would have thought I'd given each of them a million dollars. They were so excited, and the expression on their faces was precious. If I had known the sharpener would be such a hit, I would have brought a bunch of them. Later I learned that several of the teachers had never seen a pencil sharpener either.

Next I had a tour of the school classrooms. I use the term *classrooms* very loosely. It is hard to describe them; even after seeing pictures, you really had to be in one of these rooms to understand what they were like. Classes 1 through 4 were mud huts; wood cut from trees was used to create the frame. There was a hardened mud floor, and the walls had openings—just openings—for windows. I learned that glass was very expensive. The roofs were made of sheet metal that hung over the walls by several feet to protect them from rain. These roofs too had perforations to let in a bit of light without letting in rain.

I finally asked the question that had been on my mind about the "mud" walls. This was one of those questions I was afraid to ask at the risk of looking ignorant, but I needed to know: if the walls were made of mud, what happened when they got wet? Wouldn't they just fall apart? The teacher explained that the mud was mixed with cow dung, which gave the walls a much sturdier finish. I now looked at these walls in a new way! When I touched them, they did feel a bit like they were made out of concrete.

The desks were wooden and handmade by the people of Dago. They comprised a seat and then some wooden slats that angled up to another piece of wood that served as the table portion. In the younger classes, about three to four students would share a desk. In the older classes, generally two students shared a desk. In most classes there were not enough desks, so some students would just sit on the dirt floor.

The classrooms for the upper grades were similar but much sturdier, as they were made partially with concrete and brick. A large piece of slate was built into the front wall of each classroom, to be used as a blackboard. Of course there was no electricity or plumbing in the school. These were conditions that we would never see anything close to, even in the poorest areas of the United States. Thus began my education about poverty in Kenya, which gave a whole new definition to the word, and one very different from our own.

I spent a lot more time talking to the teachers. There were no formal lessons that day, as they had just finished exams, and so this was mostly a play day for the children. Soon they would be getting their test results. This led to a very interesting ceremony.

All class eight (eighth grade) students gathered as their test scores were read off. They'd been told that things were becoming more and more competitive in Kenya and so they needed to work harder. Thus the teachers assembled too, and the student with the highest score was named. This student walked to the front of the room to be the first in a line of students in front of the teachers. The younger children were all in the audience. One by one, the names of the children and their scores were read, from highest to lowest, and as their names were read, they joined the line. Finally the last few students came up, the ones who had actually failed their tests. As those students came up, the teachers would point their fingers at them and tell them that their scores were not acceptable and that they needed to work much harder. They then did some comparisons with the previous year's scores, where some went up and some went down. Then the assistant headmaster got up to talk. He told some of the low-performing students that he was ashamed of their scores because they'd gone down from previous year. He did, however, congratulate several students who had made big improvements.

As you might imagine, this was very hard for me to watch. At times I just put my head down; I couldn't look. Of course we would never embarrass our students by doing something like this in the United States. This brings up an important point that was foremost in my mind at the time. In making this trip, I had vowed to myself that I was not going to Kenya to tell the people how they should conduct themselves. I did not feel it was my place to do that. After all, who was I to tell them how to live their lives? I was there to listen to and learn from them and see how I could help.

My policy did change during future trips, as I got to know the people and the community better; however, I always have been very sensitive to this matter. On a future trip, I asked one of the teachers why he was so tough on his students, though I didn't mention any specifics, and I have to admit that his answer was a very good one. He told me that Kenya was a very poor country, and that the only way it was going to get better was if all the children there worked hard. You will also see that on future trips, several of the community leaders, primarily Duncan, encouraged me to cross that line and "strongly suggest" to them ways they could change (i.e., make education a higher priority in their homes).

Later in the day, I was asked to sit in on a meeting with some older students from class eight. The teachers were setting up special study sessions for the last two weeks of August, because soon they would be on break until the next term began in September. It was the end of July now. This would be a review session called "coaching," and it would cost two hundred Kenyan shillings, or about $2.30 in

US money. They told me that coaching was a requirement. It was not about remediation for students who had fallen behind, but rather it was further lessons from the syllabus they had been working on. The students, however, were telling me there was no way they could get this kind of money, which was intended to cover the teachers' time, since coaching was not part of their contract. The teachers were trying to impress upon the students the importance of their studies. As I recall, there were ten students lined up for coaching, so I decided I wanted to help. I had quite a bit of Kenyan money on me, so I just took some out and gave each of them enough to cover their lessons.

I then kind of got into my motivational speaking mode about the importance of working hard and getting a great education. I asked each of them to stand up and tell me what they want to do when they grew up. Their answers varied; they wanted to be teachers, doctors, nurses, lawyers, pilots, and so forth. Something I did not understand then, but clearly understand now, is that the odds of any of them achieving these goals were very slim. This kind of realization became one of the stepping-stones to start the Dago Scholarship Fund, to give some of these children the opportunity, at least, to really pursue their dreams.

When that was over, I talked about President Barack Obama and how hard he'd had to work to get to where he was, and how each of them needed to work that hard too. There were a couple of key reasons I brought up President Obama. First, of course, were his Kenyan roots; however, it went much deeper than that. As I mentioned earlier, President Obama's father was from the same tribe as these children, the Luo tribe, which was one of forty-two tribes in Kenya. The village that his father was from was not very far from Dago. This was 2009, President Obama's first year in office. There was tremendous pride in Kenya that the son of a Kenyan had risen to be the president of the United States! In Dago I saw several Obama T-shirts, caps, and bumper stickers. I was never quite sure how they arrived in Dago, but that was not really important. Later on, while I was in a much larger city, I went into a store and there was some yogurt being sold that had a picture of President and Mrs.

Obama on the packaging. I remember doubting at the time that the manufacturer had the permission of the president and the first lady to use their images, but I also had a feeling that they would not mind.

Next I shared with the teachers the lesson plans I had put together. In preparing for the trip, there was so much I had been unsure of, even though Shana Greene from Village Volunteers had been beyond superb in helping me get ready. So I'd decided that, being a teacher, I would draw up a couple of lesson plans. That turned out to be a good idea, as I will explain later.

Along with the lesson plans, I shared with the teachers a variety of maps of parts of the world, including Africa and Kenya, and a map of the Dago area from Google Earth. I talked to them about President Obama's background and shared various pictures of Chicago. They were fascinated by all of it and kept asking me questions.

I quickly learned that there were heartbreaking moments almost every hour. I could never go into all of them, but one story that stands out involves a bright young boy named Victor, who was in class six. As I go into this story, it is important for you to know that the children in Dago were told over and over not to ask volunteers like me for any money, gifts, and so forth. The adults did not want the volunteers to be bothered by children constantly asking for things. However, I learned quickly that many, in their own cute little way, would ask for things anyway.

I was walking along when I felt a little tug on my sleeve. I turned around to see a small boy who would barely even look at me. In a very quiet voice, he asked me if he could talk to me in "private." Of course I said yes. We walked to another area, where I asked him his name. In a voice that was so hushed it was hard to hear him, he said his name was Victor. And then, still barely able to look at me, he told me that he had a problem and wondered if I could possibly help.

Before I go on, I need to tell you that one of my goals in making this trip was to pick a child to sponsor—although at the time, I was not even sure what I meant by the word *sponsor*. For years I had watched TV commercials showing poor African children, and I was always tempted to send in some money. Now, while I know that most of the organizations that produce these commercials are remarkable and do great work to help these children, I always worried because of the stories that come out every now and then about how one of these "charities" is using donations to buy fancy cars, planes, mansions, and so forth. I knew how devastated I would be if someone took my money and used it for things like that. So I wanted to choose a child I had met, a child whose family and community I knew personally, and I wanted total control over the money so I would know that every penny was going to help that child. I realize that most people never have this choice, so please know that I fully support those who choose to help in any way they can through existing charities and foundations.

Now, getting back to Victor: He told me that he really wanted to get an education but both his parents were "sick." (This is how I learned that the word *sick* usually meant AIDS.) He said they would probably not live much longer, so he didn't know how he would be able to pay for school next year. I remember feeling overwhelmed by his question and the courage it had taken him to ask me. I stumbled for a moment, knowing I had to be very careful with my answer. I did not want to promise him anything I could not really follow up on.

I told him that I could not promise him anything at the moment, so I could not guarantee I would help. I told him to keep working very hard and I would talk to the teachers about it. It turned out that I would have several of these moments on my trip. They become very important moments that eventually led to the start of the Bernard and Elsie Weiss Dago Scholarship Fund. What was I going to do? Every child in Dago needed the kind of help Victor was asking me for. I knew I would have to take some serious time to think about this.

Saturday, August 1, 2009

It was Saturday morning, and a day off for us volunteers. At least that was what I'd been told, but I was not sure what that actually meant, since I did not even want a day off. I was told this because the school was not open on Saturdays and Sundays. Duncan actually described it as a day off for his family, but I never saw any difference in their activity level. This was a working farm, and of course the animals and crops did not know the difference between days. Duncan told me that this was their sabbath, their day of rest, but all day long, all the farm work, such a milking, feeding, and cleaning up, was done just like it was any other day. The real difference today was that most of the people of Dago were Seventh-day Adventists, and Saturday was their church day. More about that in a moment.

During this first trip I often thought about how, even though I was writing down a lot of what was happening each day, there were so many amazing moments, there was no way to write all of them down. Incredible things seemed to be happening every few minutes, and I worried that if I did not write about them, I would forget them.

We had no children that day to spend time with, although there were a number of children playing in the area for us to talk to. The school was closed, and the orphan girls who lived in the Dago Dala Hera Orphanage (*Dala Hera* means "Home of Love" in the Luo language) were gone. I learned about a Kenyan law that said orphans or partial orphans (having only one parent) had to spend one weekend each month "back home" with their parents or "guardians." This could mean their legal guardians, including their grandparents, aunts, uncles, and so forth. The government wanted to make sure the children kept their roots with that family, however "family" was defined. We learned that these children really did not want to go "home"; they loved being at the orphanage because life was so much better there. So late into Friday evening, most of the orphans were still there, waiting as long as they could to leave, even though many would have very long walks in the dark to get home. Several of the girls told me it would be more than an hour's walk. I did see two of the moms come pick up their children. Many of these girls had no parents and were called total orphans; girls with one parent were called partial orphans. For the girls with one parent, it had been decided by all that they were better off living in the orphanage. The orphans would not return until sometime on Sunday.

On a side note, I learned things about these children and the languages they speak, write, and read. Growing up in their homes, they learn their tribal language of Luo. Each of the forty-two tribes in Kenya has its own tribal language or, as they refer to it, their "mother tongue." When they go to school, they begin to learn the main language of Kenya, Kiswahili (the Kenyan version of Swahili), and when they get to class four, they learn English. The English comes primarily because up until 1963, Kenya was a British colony. The children are always surprised when they meet someone like me, who only knows English; they grow up in a world where almost everyone is bilingual or multilingual. I feel lucky that I only needed to learn one language, but then again, I also feel as though they are much better off because they know many languages. The older primary school children do a great job of reading, writing, and speaking English, which for me, as a teacher, reinforces the idea that when teaching other languages, we Americans really need to start when children are very little and their minds soak everything up like sponges. In this world, there are clear advantages to knowing more than one language.

I later learned that in Kenya they were trying to get people to stop speaking their tribal languages to just focus on Kiswahili and English, but this was very hard to do, especially in tiny villages like Dago. Some of the older people in Dago, who had little to no schooling, only knew Luo.

In talking with two of the girls who were sisters—the older girl was probably twelve and the younger one about eight—I learned something interesting. The older girl said to us, "I want to tell you something, but this is very private, so you cannot tell anyone else." When we assured her that she could trust us, she said that she was ashamed to say that her mother was "positive." (Their father was dead, and I assumed he died of AIDS, but I did not ask.) She went on to talk more about how ashamed she was and how she did not want people to know. We, being the volunteers, just listened and assured her that we would not tell anyone.

I need to address for you what I mean when I use the word *we*.

One of the most amazing things about my trips to Africa is the incredible people I have been able to meet from every corner of the world. Each of these people is on his or her own special journey, and their stories are all fascinating. I have learned so much from getting to meet these people in Dago and other places in Kenya, on my 2011 trip to Rwanda, and in airports. So the "we" I am referring to during this 2009 trip to Dago are various people. In a place like Dago, volunteers come and go, so you may meet some people when you first arrive who end up leaving before you do.

During this stay, as I have mentioned, I met Jyoti, an educator and attorney in London; Stephanie, a social worker in Toronto; Dariush, a college student from the United States; and Samantha, a rising sophomore in college. Each of them brought his or her own background, curiosity, and questions to all these situations. Part of the learning experience for me was just sharing all of this with them. I loved hearing their stories about their personal journeys and their reasons for coming to Kenya and what they wanted to get out of the trip.

Today I had a discussion with Duncan about religion. This is where I learned they were Seventh-day Adventists. He said that at this time of year, they did not always have church services, but instead had other meetings. There was a little church in Dago they went to. He also mentioned that local Muslims went to their mosque on Fridays, and that Muslims tended to live in the larger cities and not little villages like Dago. From my studies, I knew that most Kenyan Muslims lived in the eastern part of Kenya, near Somalia (Dago is in the far southwest).

Living in Dago, I needed to be much more cognizant of time, because everything took much longer than it did in the United States. I needed time to prepare for things that I did automatically back home. Whether it was a "shower" (really a bucket washing), going to the bathroom, brushing my teeth, or getting ready for bed, it all took a lot more time. Plus I learned that Kenyans were not real sticklers for being on time. I am a big on-time person, and having grown up with a dad who taught me that if you are not fifteen minutes early, you are late, the Kenyan sense of time was tough to get used to. It hit me that since life was so tough there and there were so many obstacles in your way, no matter what you were doing, being on time was just not as important. While this was hard for me in some ways, in many ways it was also healthy for me. This is where I began to learn that so many things that bother me in my "real life" would never bother Kenyans. While they work incredibly hard each and every day, they have a much healthier perspective on not letting things bother them. They do not get worried about so many of the things that worry me all the time!

My shower was two plastic bowls that I filled with water from a pump on the property. This water was good for washing my body or clothes, but if you drank it, you could die. The pump was about three hundred feet from the room I was staying in. After getting the water, I would walk to a little empty room in the building behind mine that had the "bathroom" and "shower." The shower was just an empty room. I would go in there with a towel, the two buckets, and some soap and shampoo. I'd wash my body and hair and then rinse with the other bucket. I would then dry myself off, and while it did not feel like the great showers I got at home, it did leave me feeling pretty clean and refreshed. It all took a long time, but it was well worth it.

Washing clothes was a similar process, involving the two buckets and some packets of liquid laundry detergent. I would sit outside and hand wash items of clothing in one bucket, rinse them in the other bucket, squeeze the water out as well as I could, and then hang them on a clothesline to dry. I felt a special kinship to my grandparents, who'd had to wash their clothes in a similar manner. There was a certain feeling of accomplishment that came from manually doing all of this instead of putting the clothes in the washing machine and the dryer and then folding them. While that was a good feeling, I still preferred using my appliances at home!

Another point I learned was that the teachers and textbooks were very direct with students on moral issues. Things we American teachers would never say to our students, the Kenyan teachers did not hesitate to say. Much of this was because the AIDS problem was so severe. They were very direct in telling students that they should not have sex until marriage. They also taught their students about the proper use of condoms, and they began having that conversation when the children were very young.

Last night during dinner at Duncan and Mama Pamela's home, they put the TV on. They got TV via satellite, powered by solar power. This was something very few people in Kenya could afford. There were two channels in Kenya, both run by the government, and much of the programming was from either the United States or England. So what was the first program we watched? The WWE—World Wide Wrestling from the United States. They only turned their TV on after dinner, which was about 10:00 p.m. Duncan, Mama Pamela, Patrick, and George were all glued to the TV every second this was on. I then mentioned to Patrick, "You do know this is all fake, just entertainment, don't you?" It led to a big discussion of the topic. In the end I was still not sure they realized it was fake, so we just moved on.

Next was the Tyra Banks show *America's Next Top Model*. The ending of the show was very upsetting because they had to cut down from six girls to five, and the girl who was cut was African, from Nigeria. Of course everyone at Duncan's house was rooting for the African girl.

Next was the news, which of course greatly interested me, the news junkie. Since we were talking, I could only watch it off and on, but the presentation of the news reminded me a lot of the BBC. It was pretty straightforward, without the casual tone of the American news. One of the big stories was about all the problems the drought was bringing to Kenya. The next story was about the government, always a matter of controversy here. Several members of parliament had called upon the prime minister to resign. Thus, their call-in survey question for that night was, "Should the Prime Minister resign?" At the end of the show, when it was time for the results, they announced that due to "technical problems," they did not have any. Patrick immediately started laughing, saying that was because the government would not let them give the results, as most of the people wanted the prime minister to resign. The family all agreed. Remember, the government owned the TV stations. Ah, politics— always interesting, wherever one is in the world.

The economics teacher in me caught another story: inflation was running at an annual rate of more than 15 percent in Kenya. This was obviously a big problem. The family had been telling me about how the prices of things like corn and sugar had almost doubled in the last year. They said they felt the rate was much higher than 15 percent; they did not feel the government was being honest. The KCB (Kenyan Central Bank) had raised interest rates with the goal of trying to get inflation below 5 percent. This was called "contractionary monetary policy," a topic I had taught many students about.

I began to understand that in a place like Kenya, if the price of corn went up by 10 percent, it could be devastating for the large number of people who were already barely surviving. However in the United States, if the price of corn went up by 10 percent, it just meant we paid a few pennies more for a box of Corn Flakes.

There was a fascinating mix of technology along with simplicity, great poverty, and harshness of life in Kenya. Some of the adults had cell phones, and this really surprised me. This part of the world, like so many, skipped landline phones and went right to cell technology. There were cell towers all over the country; there were a lot of cell calls and text messages. Many of the ads on TV and in the newspaper asked consumers to SMA something to a certain number to find out more information on a product.

I wondered how people could afford cell phones. I learned that most of the phones in Kenya came from China, which sold all its seconds and used and low-priced cell phones in Africa. Kenyans could get a phone for just a few US dollars. There was no phone "plan," as we would know it; they bought their minutes ahead of time. So when they were low on minutes, they had to buy more. They used what I would guess was a British term, "top up," for getting more minutes. In the larger towns there were many signs saying, "Top Up Here."

I was told the minutes were very inexpensive. One of my favorite pictures on this trip was a Maasai man walking alongside the road in his red robe, herding cows and talking on his cell phone. One amazing moment of history colliding with the present!

A random thought: Earlier in the morning, the teachers were looking at the lessons, maps, and pictures I had brought, including a picture of the Michael Jordan statue in front of the United Center in Chicago, and only one of the teachers had ever heard of Michael Jordan. Maybe I should not have been surprised, but I guess, being from Chicago, I was. I should have realized this when I saw George wearing a Chicago Bulls T-shirt and he said he had never heard of Michael Jordan. Sorry, Michael.

Sunday, August 2, 2009

Another gorgeous morning in Dago, Kenya. Dago had a lot of green, rolling hills and beautiful sunrises and sunsets. There were none of the wires, pollution, or other things that usually got in the way of our view back home. Last night George took us to the nearest real city, Kisii, which had about one hundred thousand people. We had some food, walked around the very crowded and noisy city, and stopped in a club. It was an amazing experience. Obviously, as the only white people there, we really stood out. People were constantly coming up to us to shake our hands, saying, "Thank you for coming to Kenya," "Welcome to Kenya," and, "We hope you love our country and come back." The sincerity of their warmth and friendliness was at times almost overwhelming.

There were some "interesting" moments. As in all Kenyan communities we visited, there were peddlers everywhere, selling about anything you could imagine. While I was talking to a man wearing a Cubs cap and selling pants, another man came up to me with all the usual greetings. He was pretty disheveled and looked like he was having tough times compared to the people in the club. He really seemed to want to talk. Pretty soon I realized that this man wanted more than the usual greeting. I had wandered about fifty feet from our group, something I was really not supposed to do, and eventually he asked me if I could help him out with money. Over the next few seconds, all kinds of nervous thoughts went through my head. I kindly told him that I could not give him money, and then I anxiously awaited his response. He just smiled, shook my hand, and said, "Thank you. Welcome to Kenya, and we hope you like our country and come back." Then he just walked away. I immediately began to wonder, if I was in a major city back in the United States and someone in this kind of situation had asked me for money, would it have turned out so well?

Peddlers were constantly coming up to me, wanting to sell me their goods, as we were waiting for our ride back to Dago. I always listened and said thank you, and they just smiled and very politely said some kind words and walked away. I was learning that Kenyans are incredibly polite people. There were notices in the club telling people what they could and couldn't do. The signs always read "Polite Notice" and not just "Notice."

The ride to Kisii was very interesting. We walked about a mile up a dirt road to the next town, Ranen, which was a bit larger than Dago. There we caught a *matatu*, which means "bus" in English, but that does not begin to describe the experience of riding in this vehicle. It was really just a large van that was in very poor condition, and I doubt it could have passed any safety inspection in the United States. Matatus stopped at most villages for people to get on and off. There were many of them on the roads, and they were constantly running. While they were really not supposed to carry more than about fourteen people, they squeezed in and easily fit more than twenty-five. Where there was a space between seats, the driver would put a small board between them so someone could sit on the board. When you got to a village for a stop, chances are you would have to get off to let other riders off, and then get back on. A typical matatu would be full of people holding suitcases, boxes, bags of grain, and so on. Also, those kinds of items would be tied to the back, sides, and top of the van, and inside the van there would be a variety of animals, such as chickens, roosters, and goats.

The matatus drove incredibly fast on roads that we would generally not call roads, as they were filled with potholes, most of them quite large. There were two employees, the driver and the guy at the sliding side door, who took the money. Usually the van was so full that the guy taking the money had to keep the door open, and he would hang out the side as the van sped down the road. Sometimes some of the passengers would also hang out the side door (but not me!). The two employees would rent the matatu for the day, and so the more people they could push in and the faster they went, the more money they could make. Riding on a matatu was definitely an experience unlike anything I had ever had back in the United States. I wanted to keep looking out the window as we sped along the road, to see everything there was to see, but I have to admit that at times, I just could not look. To be frank, there would be times in a matatu where I just looked up at the heavens and prayed to God to get me safely to my destination.

I would experience a lot more of matatus during this and future trips to Kenya. One time while sitting in a fast-moving matatu, and of course being the only white person in the van, I heard the word *muzungu* repeated several times. The comic side of me took over, and knowing that most of the people knew English pretty well, I said out loud that I was hearing the word *muzungu* a lot—did that mean I was in trouble? There was quite a bit of laughter when I said that. I was a bit worried that the question would offend them, but they saw the humor in it.

I was surprised that riding on the matatu did not bother me more than it did. I guess I had prepared myself for the fact that this would be a very different world and I just had to adjust and get used to it. I certainly learned that there were things I would accept in Kenya that I would not have accepted in my "real" life.

About halfway to Kisii (it was about an hour drive), George said we were getting out of the matatu. He was very unhappy with its condition and worked out a deal to get us on another one. The next one came right away. It was in much better condition, and it had a small TV in the front playing music videos. *Better*, of course, is a relative term. I doubt that even this new matatu could pass inspection in the United States. By the way, everywhere I went in Kenya there was music playing, one way or another. It made for a better ride— still very crowded, but nice. The road we traveled on, by the Kenyan standards we had become used to, was pretty good.

As we got closer to Kisii, we had an experience similar to the one we had coming out, but not quite as nerve-racking. We were stopped by some young men yelling at us, wanting money. They went over to the driver, and he gave them fifty Kenyan shillings (about sixty cents) and they let us go. It seems like this had become a normal part of doing business.

We were right near Kisii, on a dirt road that led into town, when we made a left turn and found that the road was completely blocked by a huge pile of dirt. The driver stopped and got out to assess the situation. He then asked all of us to get out of the matatu. He wanted to go around the dirt, but there was a pretty deep ditch he would have to go into, and he did not want to chance the maneuver with people in the matatu. We got out and he went around the dirt, and for a time I thought he would tip over, but he made it fine. We then got back in and continued to Kisii.

The day before this and again this morning, Duncan talked to me a lot about visiting the homes of some of the people who lived in Dago. We got much more serious about it this morning. He talked about several families and gave George specific instructions to make sure we met them.

I had been learning more about the tribes in Kenya. The Luo people were the second or third largest of the forty-two tribes, depending on what data you are looking at. I learned that within each tribe there were many clans. The people of Dago were part of the Kogelo clan, once again the same as President Obama's father. Mama Pamela told me that her dad was a Kogelo king. Duncan laughed and said that he'd married into royalty.

I then learned that the area where people live is pretty much divided by tribe. I was in Luo land, but there were also Maasai here and on lands occupied by other tribes. In these more modern days, the lines of the tribes are not so black and white anymore, especially in the larger cities, where people of various tribes will live in one city. We had a discussion about the Maasai people, and George mentioned that they are herders rather than farmers and tend to eat a lot more beef than the people of Dago.

As for the meals, breakfast always included bread served with jam, butter, or peanut butter. They had no way to toast it. Pancakes were quite common, although much larger than ours, and there was no syrup; they used honey or jam. (On my fourth trip, another volunteer had brought some maple syrup, which was a big hit with everyone.) There was always delicious fruit, such as mangos, bananas, or pineapples. For lunch and dinner, there was almost always a big bowl of white rice, sometimes with carrots or peas mixed in, and some kind of beef stew or chicken. Most of it I ate readily, but some of it I passed on. I ate their sweet potatoes, but unlike the sweet potatoes I was used to, these tasted just like regular potatoes to me. They served a lot of cabbage and guacamole. Their staple was the ugali that I talked about a bit earlier. It looked like a big cake, but the texture was a bit tougher than bread. It really had no taste, so they would mix it into gravy or put something like honey on it. It was very heavy and thus very filling.

Overall, the food was marvelous and plentiful. No one in this home, including the orphans, ever went hungry. Clearly this was not the case for most people who lived in the area. I kidded Mama Pamela and Duncan that I'd been hoping to lose some weight on my trip to Kenya, but with all they were feeding me I would surely gain weight instead. (Of course, there was nothing in the category of junk food or sweets.) Mama Pamela got very serious and she said she would not want to send me back to the United States having lost weight, because then the American people would think that Kenyans did not take good care of their guests. The pride of being a Kenyan really showed on her face.

Mama Pamela also told me a story about a white American

woman who had been a volunteer there about a year earlier and told her that she needed to realize that many Americans thought that all Africans went around naked and lived in trees. I could tell this was a very sensitive point with her. I debated about exactly how to respond, and finally I said that maybe there were some people who really thought this, but I thought they would constitute a very small percentage of American people.

Duncan and Mama Pamela were in charge of the Dago Kogelo Primary School and the orphanage. Mama Pamela also led a women's group and received some money from the US government to help pay for it. Mama Pamela was referred to as a "social worker," but I was not exactly sure what that meant; I knew she did not have a degree in social work. She worked with women in the community, helping them meet the multiple challenges of dealing with AIDS, raising a family, and trying to become more self-sufficient.

The orphanage and school received some donations to help provide food for the children, and Mama Pamela and Duncan's farm provided a lot of food. They asked me to help them kill a chicken for dinner by cutting its head off, but I passed on that. They also grew sugarcane, which they referred to as their "cash crop," as they made good money from it. There was a sugar factory not far from Dago where they could sell it. I saw lots of children licking sugarcane as they walked along the streets, the way American children might lick a lollipop.

Obviously none of the children had anything Americans would call a "toy." There was really no concept of a toy. Some of the boys would walk around with a long stick from a tree or a stick of sugarcane, and they would find two round things, maybe tops to plastic containers or jars, and use nails to affix them to the ends of the stick, making wheels of them. Then they would run and "wheel" this stick along. Some boys would make their toy fancier by putting a plastic container on it. I also saw boys running along with an old bicycle tire or rim, rolling it with them as they ran.

At 2:00 p.m. I was supposed to head over to the school, as the teachers had called for some special sessions with class eight. Can you imagine if I had asked my students to meet me at school at 2:00 p.m. on a Sunday for a special session? After that, the orphans would be returning, so I would head over to the orphanage.

Before I left for the school, I had an amazing experience. I was sitting on a bench under a tree by Mama Pamela and Duncan's home, finishing *Dreams from My Father,* when an eighteen-year-old named Stephen came over and began trying to read the last few pages with me. I learned later that he was trying to make some money so he could eventually go to high school, so Duncan would give him odd jobs around the farm when they come up. When Stephen saw this was a book by President Obama, he became very interested. As I mentioned earlier, this area was very proud that the son of a Kenyan was the president of the United States and thus famous and well respected.

Stephen was reading the book with me, asking for help with some big words, and this led to an amazing conversation. As we talked, I thought, *What the heck, I'm done with the book,* and so I told him that I wanted him to have it to read and share with others. He thought I wanted to lend it to him, and he promised to give it back. I told him no, it was a gift and he could keep it. He was a bit overwhelmed. I told him I could buy a new one when I got back home. When he told me it was a bit hard for him to read, I asked him if he had an English dictionary and he said yes. I told him that when he came across a word he did not know, he should just look it up in the dictionary. He smiled and said okay. He promised me he would read it and share it with others. My heart was racing and tears were flowing, as this was such an emotional experience for me. It is hard for me to come up with words to explain how it made me feel, but I can say that in addition to being an amazing teaching moment, it was a feeling of being alive in a way I had never felt before.

At 2:00 p.m., when the class eight children were supposed to start their special lessons, I arrived at school. The students were in their seats, but there was no teacher. The students asked me to teach them. I really had no clue what to do, but then I started thinking about the lessons I had prepared for this trip. I asked them a lot of questions about Kenya, and then I gave them a lesson about how Africa was colonized by Europeans in the 1800s and that was how Kenya became a British colony. I then made some comparisons to the United States, since it also had been a British colony. I went through some of the history of the United States, making a comparison between George Washington and Jomo Kenyatta, each of whom led his country in obtaining independence from the British and then became the first president of his new country. This went on for about ninety minutes, and to my amazement, the students were taking notes and asking great questions.

When the teacher came in during my lesson on social studies, he just sat in the; back and listened. I felt pretty awkward and told him that I was just filling in until he got there, and I wanted him to begin his lesson. I did not want him to think I had tried to replace him. He seemed to be very happy with what I had done, and to this day I have no idea why he was so late.

The teacher then started his lesson about the history of Kenya from 1895. I was wondering if he was talking about this because of what I had said, or if this had been his plan all along. He began teaching about the Berlin Conference and how Africa was divided up among the European powers. He covered the material and wrote on the chalkboard, and the students took notes about Kenyan history until its independence in December 1963. He covered a lot of detail, much of it new information for me. The students were incredibly attentive and again asked a lot of questions. I was very interested to watch him teach and interact with his students. The bare essentials of the room almost became invisible to me as I got wrapped up in what was happening in the classroom. He went on for almost two hours, and the students were very patient; they were so incredibly eager to learn and so appreciative of any knowledge they gained. I could not imagine my American students being this patient.

I spent several hours at the orphanage. I'd learned from Duncan the day before that it was built a few years earlier, when a Peace Corps worker, who had spent a summer in Dago and saw firsthand that AIDS was leaving a lot of children with no parents, was able to get $20,000 of Peace Corps money to build it. We played with the girls as the mothers cooked dinner. The girls sang and danced and had a lot of fun.

I was able to talk to my wife, Chris, on the phone that night, which really made me feel good and extra pumped up!

Monday, August 3, 2009

It was another gorgeous morning in Dago. I washed my hair and semi-showered. I would be going to school soon, but then at 10:00 a.m. I would be getting on a motorbike to go with Mama Pamela for her meeting with her women's group. I was told it would be about a forty-five minute ride.

The night before at the orphanage, I'd met a girl named Milka. She was fifteen and an orphan, but now she went to high school. She was incredibly personable and talkative. She loved Dago and lived right near it. She especially loved coming around to help out with the orphans. When she left, she said she had to go home to do her homework. Before that, she handed me a letter that she had written. On the bottom line of the letter, she asked me for money to help with her school costs. This was part of my education about the reality of high school in Kenya and the costs involved. As I mentioned, asking for this kind of thing was quite common, and it was so frightening to me that all these bright young children lived in constant fear that they might not be able to continue their education because of a lack of money.

Milka showed me a big folder that contained much of her schoolwork, and in it I saw her school bill. It showed that the government would pay about ten thousand Kenyan shillings (about $112), and she had to come up with about seven thousand shillings (about $80). Later on I learned that while these bills showed what the government would pay, the reality was that the government never paid it. These costs were just for part of the school year, by the way. For the students' families, this was an incredible amount of money.

I arrived at the school at 8:00 a.m. and talked with the teachers.

Then there was the flag-raising ceremony in the center of the school grounds. I learned that certain students were picked for this, and it was a great honor. The students marched in and raised the Kenyan flag, and then they sang the Kenyan national anthem. Then the assistant headmaster, Henry, spoke to the students, who were assembled by class. Henry told the students that he was quite upset, as this was the last week of classes before the Kick It in Kenya tournament and there were many students missing. He later said to the students that just because exams were over, some students thought they did not need to come to school. Later I saw Henry making calls on his cell phone, looking for some of the students. I was a bit confused, because most of the students were not at school.

The first lessons were supposed to start at 8:20 a.m. I made my way to the class eight room; because I'd worked with those students on Sunday, I thought I would go to that class. Each class stayed in the same room all day, and the teachers of the various subjects would move from room to room. The older the students were, the nicer their classrooms were. However, I use "nicer" in a relative manner, as the rooms were made of mud, some concrete, and bricks, with a metal roof full of small holes, and dirt floors. The desks were handmade and in very poor condition.

When I came in and sat down, the students all said hi to me and asked me to stand up and teach them a lesson, since no teacher had arrived. Of course I was concerned and confused about why there was no teacher. I told them I did not want to interfere, but they said I should go ahead and teach. I realized it was time to take my teaching skills and wing it.

I decided to give them a review of their lesson on Kenyan independence for a start. In my mind I was panicking a bit, not knowing what to do. I had prepared some other lessons, but they were locked away in the headmaster's office. By this time, another teacher had heard me talking and brought me some chalk. Between my loud voice and the fact that the school was all out in the open, it was easy to hear me. One of the students erased the chalkboard, and I was on my way.

So I again went through a comparison of the histories of Kenya and the United States. I added to this some points about the Native Americans, trying to help the students understand the similarities. My main goal was to help them understand the key point that we both had been colonies of England and had to fight for our independence. The United States had been independent for more than two hundred years, while Kenya had been independent for less than fifty. I kept asking students a lot of questions so it was not just me talking; they asked lots of terrific questions too. Next I went into the history of African Americans and talked about how Africans were kidnapped and brought to the United States and sold as slaves. I talked a bit about the 1896 *Plessy v. Ferguson* Supreme Court decision, which created the entire "separate but equal" concept, and how this did not change until *Brown v. Board of Education* in 1954. I wanted them to understand a bit about the African American struggle for equality in the United States.

About an hour had gone by, and it was past break time, but their teacher had not yet arrived. I told them I had to leave to go with Mama Pamela, and I gave them a break.

I walked to Mama Pamela's house while she was getting ready. We left her home about 10:45 a.m. and made the mile walk on the dirt road to Ranen. Mama Helda, one of the mothers who helped out in the orphanage, came with us. In Ranen we met up with two other women who were also helpers, as they were coming with us too. We hopped onto a matatu and rode about thirty minutes to the town of Awendo. We stopped there, and Mama Pamela bought us all lunch at a restaurant. I had a cold bottle of Coke, the first cold beverage I'd had since Nairobi.

Then the trip became a lot more interesting. Mama Pamela said we had to go to the "interior," and no matatus went there. Here is where the motorbikes came in. There were young men who made a living by giving people rides on their motorbikes to places where matatus did not go. Soon each of us was on the back end of a motorbike and on our way. The first part of the journey was on a paved road, but most of it was on very poor dirt roads. I hung on tight to the driver.

We rode for about thirty minutes until we reached a little village. There was a group of women playing netball and being coached by a man who was preparing them for the tournament coming up in a week. The players were the mothers in the community. I learned that netball was a British game similar to basketball, but played outside, on grass. The women could pass the ball but not dribble it. At each end of the playing field, there was a piece of wood about eight feet high with a rim attached to the top for the basket. Since there was no backboard, it was very difficult to score. I also learned that this game was played only by girls and women, while football (soccer) was played only by boys and men. This was part of their very traditional society, and these "rules" were not challenged.

At a later time in my trip, I mentioned to a group of men that in the United States, girls and women played football (soccer). They were absolutely shocked, and one of them actually said, "Girls cannot play football."

Next the women gathered in a building and watched some music videos while discussing several items. There was a video in Kiswahili that must have gone on for twenty minutes, and it seemed as though the last word of every line was *Obama*. There were video clips that included President and Mrs. Obama along with their daughters. By now it had started to rain heavily, and so Mama Pamela led everyone to an open area that was covered. She then led a more formal meeting, mixing in some English so I could understand a bit of what she was talking about.

It was here that I learned much more about what Mama Pamela did. There were forty-five women in the group; they were representatives of this district, or what we would call a county. Five of them were called "social workers," but I learned this did not really mean they had a college degree in social work; they were just looked at that way. However, one of the women was going to college to study social work. Mama Pamela was in charge of the entire project, which was funded by the United States government. Their job was to reach out to all the families in their area to try and get them whatever help they needed, such as clothes, blankets, bedding, food, or medicine.

Mama Pamela then gave them what I would call a motivational speech. She was an incredibly strong leader and a very positive role model for the women of this community. She clearly let the women know about things she was not happy with in regard to their work. She mentioned that several of them were not doing their job well, that they were not reaching all the families in the community and that they must do that. When Mama Pamela spoke, she had the full attention of every woman in attendance.

Mama Pamela then asked me and Samantha, one of the ladies she had brought, to speak to the women. She wanted us to introduce ourselves and give them advice. After Samantha spoke, I introduced myself, using the new Luo name Duncan had given me, Brett Okinyi Wuid Dago. "Okinyi" was because of the time of the morning I was born, and the rest meant I was from Dago. I learned this was the way all babies were named.

Now, I really had no idea what to say to the women. I told them how important I thought their work was, and that it was crucial for them to make sure each child in their community got as much education as possible, because education was the key to their success in life and in improving Kenya. I also talked about the importance of proper nutrition, saying that each day, the children needed to eat good, healthy food. I explained that children with proper nutrition would learn more in school.

After this, Mama Pamela took out some money to start the process of giving each woman her "stipend." Mama Pamela described it as a small monetary token to show appreciation to the women for the work they did. The money came from USAID. As the money was passed out, each of the helpers talked with the mentors for a final meeting.

Near the end of all this, I had a woman tap me on the shoulder and say she needed to ask me something. She told me that she did not have a husband and asked me if I could give her one hundred Kenyan shillings (about $1.20). I told her that I was sorry but I could not do that, and I walked away. I knew that I would get asked for a lot of things, and as tough as it was to say no, I had to. A couple of women nearby who heard this conversation were clearly upset with her and let her know that. This was another heart-wrenching moment.

It rained hard through most of the meeting, but the rain had stopped by the time we were ready to head back home to Dago. Luckily, we were able to have our meeting inside a pretty large room. Mama Pamela had arranged for the motorbikes to come back, and so we hopped back on the bikes and started the trip home. Because of all of the rain, the dirt road was very muddy and slippery. This made for a very interesting ride that I considered pretty dangerous. On a motorbike, you always had to hold onto the driver to stay on the back. I knew I needed to hold on a little tighter now.

Back at Awendo, where we'd originally gotten on the motorbikes, we now got on a matatu and headed back to Dago with a bit of daylight left. When we reached Ranen, Mama Pamela bought a few things at the market and then we started walking back to Dago. It is about a mile walk, and it was incredibly muddy and slippery; there were many times I almost fell down. It was also dark by now, so I was doing this in total darkness. Back in Dago, I changed my clothes, which had become quite dirty. I washed up and walked back over to Mama Pamela and Duncan's home for dinner and some great conversation.

Tuesday, August 4, 2009

When I arrived at the school around 8:30 a.m., only one teacher and about half the students were there. The teacher asked the students to clean up around the school. They took whisk brooms, and some just took branches with leaves from the trees to make whisk brooms, and they swept up the grounds. They also went around picking up branches that had fallen to the ground during the storm. I assumed they would use them in fires for heat and cooking.

Lessons started around 9:00 a.m. I went to class eight to see the children, whom I had gotten to know by now. Their teacher was not there, so they asked me to teach a lesson. Of course I had not prepared anything and still did not have the materials I'd brought. I decided to write a question on the chalkboard: "What needs to be done to make Kenya a better country?" Then I wrote down their ideas. They said things like ending corruption (which was very widespread), better schools, and stopping war (they meant fighting between tribes). I added to the conversation things like safe water, indoor plumbing, electricity, and so forth. I learned that they really understood how big a problem corruption was in Kenya. I also learned that the lack of indoor plumbing was not something they seemed to perceive as a problem.

We had a great discussion on all of these issues. The students were very talkative and open about them. I later learned that their teacher never showed up, so after I left they had no lessons for the rest of the day. There were things that happened in Kenya that I just did not understand and really did not get answers to.

Next Samantha and I met up with Mama Pamela for our trip to the nearest medical facility/hospital in Awendo. The purpose was for Mama Pamela to pay the bill for the orphan children who got services there. She paid all the medical bills for the orphans and their relatives with money she got from USAID.

We walked on the mile–long dirt road to Ranen to catch a matatu, and then we were on our way. The ride to Awendo was about twenty minutes. When we got off, we had to walk a few blocks down a dirt road to get to the hospital, which was a collection of several white buildings. There were separate areas for women, men, and children. Mama Pamela introduced us to several people who worked at the hospital, including the doctor who oversaw the facility. We had the chance to sit in her office and ask some questions. As one would expect, she told us she had nowhere near enough staff or supplies. She explained what a difficult situation she had. One big problem was that most people would never even make it to the hospital for help, either because they were stubborn or because they lived so far away that the walk was too much for them.

We walked around various parts of the hospital, and it was nowhere near what we would call a medical facility. It was not very clean, and parts were just plain dirty. Then I experienced one of the most moving moments of my life, which brought me to tears. We were in the HIV/AIDS ward—of course, that disease was a major problem in Kenya and much of sub-Saharan Africa—and I walked into a room where a grandmother was holding her little grandson in her arms. The baby was a year and a half old, but he was the size of a newborn. He'd been born with AIDS and was near death. There really are no words to describe the scene.

I started wondering about the baby's mother, and then when I walked into the next room, I had my answer. The mother was lying in a bed, near death herself from AIDS. This meant that soon the grandmother would be the only one of the three left. I was in tears, and my body was shaking. I had been very close to both my parents in the closing months and days of their lives; however, I cannot compare how I felt at this moment to anything I had ever been through. For me this was an entirely new experience; sadly, for the people in this part of the world, it was just a normal part of life.

Next we needed to help Mama Pamela and her friend with the main mission of the day, paying the bill. She wanted to make sure she was paying only for the services that were actually provided to the Dago people. She also needed to make sure the charges were added up correctly. We needed to match a card filled out for each visit with the visits that were recorded on a spreadsheet. If there were any incorrect charges, Mama Pamela couldn't pay for them, because she would not be reimbursed by USAID. This was a very tedious process, and we came up with a number of items that were not recorded properly, so Mama Pamela did not pay for them. Here is where I learned that Mama Pamela was incredibly well organized, great with detail, very tough, and determined that things would be done right.

Mama Pamela next met with the man who ran the business part

of the hospital. He needed to finalize the transaction with his official stamp. When this was completed, we were on our way back to the town center of Awendo. Mama Pamela needed to go to the bank to actually transfer the money to the hospital. Unfortunately, by the time we arrived at the bank, it was already closed. Mama Pamela would have to do this tomorrow.

As we were going down the hill to the center of Awendo, I met a man named Dick. He was about my height and on the husky side; thus he was much bigger than most Kenyan men. He was dressed very sharply and was very friendly and talkative. He walked with me down the hill, wanting to know a lot about me. As we talked, I learned that he was a businessman and his wife was a secondary school teacher. They had three children. I asked him about his business, and he said that he sold clothes that were seconds or used. He would buy large boxes of them in Nairobi and then hire peddlers to sell them on the street. I asked him how business was going, and he said very badly. Between Kenya's bad economy, which was getting worse and worse, and its current inflation problem, people had very little money to spend. He then wanted to take a picture with me and asked me to write down my name and e-mail address for him. He promised he would e-mail me, but he never did.

Since the bank was closed and it was about 4:00 p.m. and we had not eaten since breakfast, Mama Pamela took us to the same restaurant where we'd eaten the day before. It was pretty nice by Kenyan standards, although it had a fairly limited menu. I had goat for lunch. Yes, I actually ate goat, something I never thought I would do. It was very good. Not like chicken—more like beef.

After we ate, we walked a few blocks to what looked like an apartment building that was several stories high. It turned out it was a combination of residences and businesses. We walked up to the second floor to a business that had electricity; it sold computer services and had a copy machine so you could pay for copies. Mama Pamela needed made some copies, and then the ladies who were her helpers arrived and they sat in the store to discuss their business. There was a balcony in front of every unit, so I stood out there to take pictures and wave to people. Right about then, it started raining very hard. Because of the terrible drought Kenya has been suffering from, the rain was very welcome. I was told there were parts of Kenya that had not had any significant rain for years.

We took a matatu back to Ranen, but we still had the mile of dirt (now mud) ahead of us to get back to Dago. By this time it was dark and raining very hard. Mama Pamela tried to pay a taxi driver to take us back to Dago, but he refused for fear his car would get stuck in the mud. Mama Pamela bought a flashlight, or what they call a "spotlight." I chuckled at the word, assuming this must be British terminology. So we carefully headed home. I am not the most coordinated person in the world, and I was having trouble not falling flat on my face. To my amazement, I watched many Kenyan women zooming past me with very large bundles balanced on their heads. I could not understand how they could do this, even on a smooth surface during nice weather. Watching them do it now, in the mud and ruts, was one of the most astonishing things I had ever seen.

Wednesday, August 5, 2009

By 7:00 a.m. I had been up for a while and had given myself a complete tub shower/bath and washed my hair. While this was not as good as the nice long shower I would take when I got home, I did feel extremely clean and refreshed. Also I hand washed the pants I had worn for the past two days to get the mud off and get them reasonably clean. I hung them up on the line, along with my towel and washcloth, to let them dry. I also hung up the clothes I'd worn the night before, which were still very wet from all the rain. I was so busy the day before that I had not been able to write at all.

Life here forced you to give a great deal of thought to every basic necessity. Everything took longer and you had to plan out the logistics carefully. It was a very hard life, and yet they made it pretty easy for us as volunteers. We got three excellent meals each day. By Kenyan standards, we had incredible accommodations.

I went to the school about 8:00 a.m., and once again there were many students but few teachers. I did a lesson with the class eight students where I asked them to name countries. We made a very long list. Then I started naming some African countries and asked them to tell me what they know about them. They were very good at telling me the capitals and other key facts. I used this occasion to talk to them about a topic I spent a lot of time on with my own students, the Rwandan genocide of 1994 and the current genocide in Darfur, Sudan. I learned they knew some things about Rwanda but not much about Darfur.

We thought there was going to be a school closing ceremony when our lessons were done, but the headmaster started a meeting with the teachers and asked us to come back for the ceremony at 1:00 p.m. When we arrived, there were many adults sitting in chairs across from the soccer field, so we headed over there. When we got closer, I saw a couple of men in military uniforms. As we approached them, I recognized one of them as a man we'd met the day before. His nametag said "Chief." He was about six feet tall and very well built, a bit like an NFL linebacker. This made him stand out from most Kenyan men, who are typically quite slender. He shook my hand, welcomed me with a big smile, and thanked me for coming to the meeting. To be frank, I did not even know I was going to a meeting.

It turned out this was a community meeting, and the community was invited there by the chief. I learned that chiefs were appointed by the government to manage communities. I sat down at one of the desks that had been brought down from the school. A bunch of chairs faced the audience. In these seats were the chief, the assistant chief, and the community elders. A couple of women were among the community elders, and the chief came up to me to talk because he wanted me to see that in Kenya they included women as part of the decision-making process. He said that in Kenya, they were "gender sensitive." To be frank, this was not very convincing.

The meeting began with the chief explaining to the volunteers in English that the meeting would be in Luo, their tribal language, since many adults did not speak English. He also told us we were

51

free to take pictures. It was as if he'd read my mind, and so I started taking lots of pictures.

Then the official meeting began. The assistant chief talked for about ten minutes and then introduced the chief. The chief then talked for about ten minutes. He was a big man, and he carried this big stick—it looked like metal—as he walked along. He was always waving it. He was a very imposing man to begin with, and he certainly wanted to add to this image. For the next hour or so, I watched a number of the elders and community people speak in Luo. The audience had grown to about fifty men and women. After Duncan spoke, I saw things happening over at the school. I did not want to miss the closing, so I headed back over there.

I learned that this was the close of the term, and that the students would have a couple of weeks off before the start of the next one. The students were assembled in a large room that was actually two classrooms; a room divider opened up to make it one large room. This was the same room where they had been singing and praying the previous Friday morning. They sat by class levels, with the teachers up front, facing the students. Each teacher gave a report for his or her students. Next the headmaster and assistant headmaster spoke. Then, starting with class one, they read off the names of the top three students in each class based on exam scores. Then each student shook the hands of the volunteers and then the teachers. When they made it to classes seven and eight, they did what I'd seen done with class eight earlier: from top to bottom, each student was called up based on his or her score. At the end of the line were the students who had not passed the exam. The teachers clearly saw this as a way to motivate the students who had not done well. It was very tough for me to watch, as in the United States we would never humiliate students in this manner. However, I did not see my role as telling them how to run their schools, so I just stayed quiet and watched.

In the lower grades, the girls clearly did better than the boys, but by the time we got to the upper grades, that trend had reversed. The assistant headmaster was kidding the female volunteers about this in a way we did not understand, and it was really bothering them. They were very critical of the girls who did not do well. It was getting a bit uncomfortable. Next they asked each of us to say something to the students. I congratulated all of them and encouraged each of them to work hard, and I told the students who did not do well that they could still turn it around with hard work. Next Samantha and Stephanie spoke, and they directly addressed the gender issue. They told all the girls that they were just as good as the boys and should never let anyone tell them differently. When they finished, the assistant headmaster, Henry, translated it all into Luo so the little children could understand.

Then Henry proceeded to give another talk in both Luo and English, and some of the words he included told me they'd gotten the message from Samantha and Stephanie. I could tell they were not exactly used to women speaking out strongly on an issue. They told the students that while they were home to help their parents with planting and other chores around the home, they should also make sure they took time to read. Most of the students were off until September, but class six and class eight would be back for special lessons during the last two weeks of August.

Then each teacher was to meet his or her students in their classroom to pass out their report cards. Henry, who was also the class eight teacher, asked me to give the report cards to his students, since I had been spending a lot of time with them. This was a big honor, and it was a lot of fun. So I walked over to the class eight room, and one by one I shook hands with the students and gave them their report cards. We then took a bunch of "photos," as the students called them.

There were about thirty students in class eight. The numbers in the lower classes were much larger, indicating that many students left school before reaching the upper grades. The cost of school seemed to be part of the problem. While the government paid most of the cost of primary education, there were still lots of different fees that had to be paid. Even though students were not supposed to ask us for money, we were constantly being asked by students for money to help them pay school fees. They were always very polite and respectful when they asked. Clearly, each of them lived with the fear every day that they may have to quit school because of a lack of money.

As always, dinner at Mama Pamela's and Duncan's was wonderful and provided a lot of laughter. The day before, Dariush had joined us as a volunteer. He was a college student from the United States who had just spent two weeks with the Maasai people. He had a very interesting background, as his dad was from Iran and his mom was from Switzerland. His main job there would be to help out the Dago football (soccer) team for Kick It in Kenya, a brand-new tournament where young men from various villages would compete against one another.

This was more of a relaxing day. Around 10:30 a.m., we walked over to the orphanage to see the orphan girls before they went home for the break. We spent a few hours with them. They were cleaning the orphanage, so we helped out. They sang a number of songs, and then Mama Helda asked each of us to give a good-bye speech to them. I really wanted them to hear from me the kind of words they had heard from Samantha and Stephanie earlier that morning. I wanted them to hear a man tell them that if they worked hard, they could become anything they wanted to be, and that they should never let anyone, especially a man, tell them they couldn't do something. Mama Helda translated our words into Luo so the younger girls could understand. We then said good-bye but told them we hoped to see them at the tournament.

Also, a big event happened this morning: I shaved for the first time since leaving home. While I do not have a heavy beard, it was getting pretty long and scratchy. It comes in pretty white, so I felt like I was beginning to look a bit like Santa Claus. I hadn't brought a mirror with me, and that was why I had not shaved yet. I know lots of guys can shave without a mirror, but for some reason I need one. When I asked if anyone had a mirror I could borrow, I received some empty stares. Finally George said he might have one. He went to a back room, and I heard a lot of noise. He was clearly looking through a bunch of things. He came back and handed me a side-view mirror from a car. I asked him how he got it, but I never really received an answer. I'd brought some cheap blades, so it took a long time to shave off all the hair, but it felt so good.

I also learned something very interesting: when a baby was born, they gave it a last name based on whatever the mom and dad decided. It could be based on something like the time of day the baby was born, or the season. Thus everyone in the family had a different last name. I learned more about their names over the next few days, and it became really confusing. Babies also got a Christian name and what I would call a first name. As I write this, almost seven years after my first trip, I am still pretty confused about names in Kenya.

By 7:15 p.m., it had been raining very hard for about an hour. While I was nice and safe and dry, Mama Pamela was still out doing her important work. I'd had more time to reflect that day than any day since I arrived in Kenya. Every second there had been amazing. These people had so few of the things we Americans think are important, but they felt so blessed. They were incredibly poor, yet they seemed truly happy. They were the happiest, most polite people I had ever met. Their lives were incredibly hard, yet they were filled with such hope. Could they learn a lot from our world? Of course they could. However, we could and needed to learn so much from them too. They had kept values, such as a sense of community, that we seemed to have lost. They were always there to help others in their community. They had an appreciation of life that was hard for us to understand. I hoped I was smart enough to incorporate what I was learning here into my everyday life.

On this day, like most days, I felt I had far more to write than I had time to write. Every second was so new, special, and unique.

Friday, August 7, 2009

By 8:00 a.m., I had washed my hair and cleaned up a bit (at least by Kenyan standards). It was a bit cloudy, and the coolest it had been since I arrived. "Cool" here seemed to be somewhere in the fifties back home. I put on a hoodie I had brought and went on with my day. For the Kenyan people, though, it was quite cold.

Duncan, Mama Pamela, and their daughters, Christine and Susan, were all working hard at their chores. I felt a bit guilty sitting there by the water well, writing. I jotted down a quick story from yesterday, when Stephanie and Jyoti visited the nearby home of a girl named Milka and met her baby sister. Her name was Michelle Obama. Also, I'd met several boys over the past few days who had the name Obama.

The night before I was able to read a newspaper for the first time since I arrived in Kenya. It was a local Kenyan paper, and one of the big stories was about Secretary of State Hillary Clinton being in Nairobi for the African Trade Conference. She gave a very stern lecture to the Kenyan government on the need for democratic reforms and ending corruption. From my time in Kenya, I can see that while we certainly have plenty of our own corruption here in the United States (and especially in my home of Illinois), corruption in Kenya is a major problem at many levels. Reducing corruption there is a major task that is desperately needed.

At 5:00 p.m. I had just come back from a funeral a few blocks away. It turned out that the man who died was the brother of Henry, the assistant headmaster from the school. Later I learned that he actually was Henry's half-brother. With so many blended families because of AIDS and other illnesses, and with some families still practicing polygamy, there were a lot of half- and step-siblings. I shook Henry's hand and expressed my condolences. I spent about two and a half hours at the funeral, but the total event, I was told, had been going on for days. Mama Pamela and Duncan's youngest son, Felix, who was fifteen, came with me to the funeral, which was held outdoors, right by the home of the deceased. He would be buried on his own property. There was no concept of a cemetery here.

When I arrived at the front of the home, there was a canvas held up by tree branches to protect people from the sun and rain. However, there were far more people than there was canvas. One of my concerns in going to the funeral was that I did not want to interfere with the ceremony in any way. Whenever a muzungu like me showed up for something, it tended to make a big splash. When we arrived at the funeral, it was already well underway and very solemn. While it was crowded, people insisted that Felix and I sit up front. They were always so polite and respectful to visitors.

For the next two hours, the man who was something like a moderator got up to speak, as did various friends and relatives. They were using a portable microphone system with a speaker powered by a car battery. Many people got up and moved around. Lots of men and women made a point of coming up to me to shake my hand and say hello. While the talking was going on, I noticed that the coffin was on a pedestal of sorts in front of the home. People were constantly going up to the coffin to pray, and some of them would lift the top of the front part of the coffin for a moment or two. This seemed to be their version of an open coffin.

Also, while Mama Pamela had asked me not to take pictures, out of respect, there was a man who took many pictures through the entire event. He seemed to be the official funeral photographer. Finally we all moved to the side of the house, where a big hole had been dug for the coffin. People stood around this area while the coffin was pulled over with ropes and lowered into the hole. After that, several men filled in the hole with dirt. During all of this, there were prayers being led by a deacon from their church. This was an incredible experience for me.

Saturday, August 8, 2009

During the night we had some more rain, although not as much as the night before. The Kenyans were all happy, because these rains meant they could start their planting. Everyone here was working very hard, even though it was Saturday, which was their sabbath. Try telling the "day of rest" story to cows, goats, sheep, and chickens.

The day before, we'd had a number of area children once again asking us if we could help pay for their schooling. It was so hard to tell each one we would see what we could do. Of course, we would have liked to help every one of them. These people understood far better than most people in the world the importance of an education.

And for them, the consequences of life without an education were drastic. The lack of an education here meant a life of extreme poverty far worse than most people in the developed world could imagine. These children were so passionate about how an education would not only improve their lives but also make Kenya a better country.

There was something that did bother me about these awesome Kenyans. To a certain extent, everything was "okay" with them. They were so nice and polite that, if someone was late, it was "okay." If someone did not do something they were supposed to do, it was "okay." This went on and on. They did have some pretty strict lines they drew on some issues, such as HIV/AIDS and polygamy, because of the tremendous negative ramifications they had had on their country. I guess in my world, not everything was "okay." I did love and respect how kind, open, and flexible Kenyans were, but was it too much?

We were supposed to be doing some home visits, and I was hoping this would happen today. My time in Dago was winding down, and I had some mixed emotions. Obviously I couldn't wait to get back home and see my wife, children, family, and friends. I couldn't wait to get back to my life. I did miss the many comforts and conveniences of home, and I was not sure yet how this trip would change my life. When I got home, I would need to work on catching up with my life via e-mails, texts, phone, and so forth. And my first day back to school would be just ten days away, so I would need to get busy with that. I was thinking how glad I was that I'd worked hard during the summer before this trip, so that I would be close to being ready for school when I got back. Also when I got back, I would need to type up my journal; I had been handwriting everything in a notebook. I would organize my pictures and use my Wikispaces page to share with family, friends, coworkers, and students stories about my two-and-a-half-week journey to Kenya. I was sure this would have an impact on my life.

This was a house visit day and of course a day of more incredible experiences. First we walked to the home of two orphan girls we had spent some time with, Sharon and Faith. It took about ten minutes to get to their home, one of two mud huts with thatched roofs. These roofs were atypical; most of the roofs were sheet metal. We were invited inside, where we met Sharon and Faith's brothers and sisters. There were five children in this family, and later we realized that there were also five more children. The father's brother had passed away and his wife was very "sick," so they had taken in the couple's five children. It turned out that one of the brothers here was Stephen, the young man I'd given the book to. Right away he came up to me to tell me that the words were very hard but he was trying his best to read the book. I was thrilled that he was trying so hard. We met the mother and father and took pictures. The father was talkative and friendly. These twelve people lived in a mud hut that was, like most huts, smaller than most people's living rooms back home.

Next we moved on to Mama Helda's home. Her son, Kevin, was someone I'd gotten to know pretty well in working with class eight. Mama Pamela met us at the home, and we had a nice long conversation there about many topics. Mama Pamela asked a lot of questions, particularly about my thoughts on the funeral I'd gone to the day before. I told her that it was very similar to funerals I had been to in the United States. We then had a conversation about funeral customs.

Mama Pamela mentioned that one of the most frustrating challenges faced by her women's group was that the poorest families tended to have the most children. I chuckled a bit and told her that there was the same problem in the United States, and really around the world. She seemed relieved that this was not just a Kenyan problem. We then had a great discussion about why poor families around the world tended to have a lot of children. Of course, one of the issues in Kenya was the high death rate of children, and the other was the need to have children working in the fields so families could make enough money to survive. We talked a lot about how as the AIDS rate came down and farming became more efficient and less dependent on children's labor, the birthrate would decline in these families. I shared with her some of the history of the United States and how families today were much smaller than they used to be.

Mama Pamela then asked me if we had poor people in the United States. I told her yes, and she seemed a bit surprised. I knew that Kenyans tended to view everyone in the United States as wealthy. I explained, though, that our definition of poverty was very different from theirs, and that most of our poor people owned cars and lived in homes with electricity, plumbing, and heat and air conditioning. It was very difficult for someone in Kenya to understand how someone with these kinds of amenities could be called poor.

Mama Helda fed us a lunch of white rice and lentils. She also had bottles of Coke, Sprite, and Fanta that we could choose from. They were warm but very nice to have. Her home was a couple of mud huts, but the main one was much larger than most. Just she and her son, Kevin, lived there. She had several older children who lived on their own. There were two "bedrooms" that were divided from the main room by sheets that hung from the wall. She explained that she'd built the home a few years earlier, after her husband died. She said they purposely built the extra space so that children from the neighborhood could sleep at her house when they needed a place to stay. Mama Helda was very much a caretaker, both at the girls' orphanage and throughout the community.

She showed us a package of pictures she had kept from over the years. We saw pictures of her husband, her children when they were younger, and other friends and relatives. Next we took about a ten-minute walk to the home of Mama Maria, another mom who helped out at the orphanage. I was told she was about seventy years old and had not been feeling well the past few days, so she had been resting. I was interested in meeting her, as there were few people over their midforties in the village. While she was extremely ill that day, normally she had a lot of energy. Only two of her ten children were still alive, but she did have grandchildren. We met her youngest son, Peter, who was twenty-one. Her home was a small mud hut with just the main room and a bedroom. The two rooms were divided by a mud wall. Like most people in the area, she used a kerosene lamp as her only source of light, although she did show us a switch that turned on three little lights in the ceiling. The light was very minimal, but she was very excited about them. They were powered by a solar panel. Mama Maria spoke very little English, so Mama Pamela and Mama Helda had to translate.

Our last home visit was about a ten-minute walk, and we saw several children we knew at the home. There was no father, and the lady with them was the sister of the mother, who was not there because she was "sick."

We then headed back to Mama Pamela and Duncan's home, where I took a bit of a nap and started my writing. The next morning we had to be at the town center to see the Dago teams play soccer and netball in the tournament. It was supposed to start at 10:00 a.m., but from what I understood, like most things in Kenya, it would actually start much later than scheduled. I had also learned that a major reason for the tournament was to give out AIDS information and have a place where people could be tested.

Sunday, August 9, 2009

Today was the start of the tournament. After breakfast, we helped Patrick with some of the used uniforms and socks that would be given out as prizes. Around 10:00 a.m., Patrick drove us over to the field at the village of Yago, just a few minutes from Dago. There were a variety of things happening as a part of the opening ceremony. I was asked to take part in a ceremony of shaking hands with all of the players who would play in the first soccer game, including the Dago team. Then I was given the great honor of kicking the ball out to the middle of the field to get things started. This was the equivalent of the honor of throwing out the first pitch at a baseball game.

When the game started, it was quite warm, and many people had gathered and were very enthusiastic. The field, while much better than the field by the Dago orphanage, was still far from the quality of a soccer field in the United States. It did have goals on both ends, but they'd been built from trees, with netting attached.

The Dago team won seven to one, a very lopsided score. Near the end of the game, the Dago women began their match on the nearby netball field. (By the way, in Kenya, as in England, people do not say "game"; they say "match.") They played a group of women who seemed much younger, but it was a very good match. Dago ended up losing by one point.

I got a ride back to my "home," as several hours out in the hot sun with nothing to drink took its toll on me. I was ready to go home. Tomorrow would be my last full day in Dago, and I would use it to begin the process of packing up, cleaning my room, spending more time at the tournament, and getting ready to head to Nairobi on Tuesday morning so I could start the journey home.

Monday, August 10, 2009

I spent the bulk of the day at the second day of the tournament, even though neither of the Dago teams was playing. The tents that were supposed to be up yesterday were up today.

When we arrived, the Kenyan Red Cross had a tent set up. We then met the people who were going to be doing the HIV/AIDS testing. A counselor named Alex gave us a very detailed explanation of the AIDS problem in Kenya and what the Red Cross would be doing at the tournament. We learned at the end of the day that they tested more than three hundred people. This Province of Nyanza was one of eight provinces in Kenya, and almost 16 percent of its people were known to have AIDS. Alex told us the number was really much higher, as there were still many people who had never been tested, either because they were too stubborn or because they lived so far from a testing place that they did not want to make the trip.

I also spent some time in a room where they were giving various medicines and vitamins to moms for their young children. Patrick had told us earlier that morning that at the last minute he'd had to pay these people an extra five hundred Kenyan shillings (about $6.50) to come out. I knew they had paid them already. So was this another example of Kenyan corruption, or a legitimate fee? I was just not sure.

Tuesday, August 11, 2009

After breakfast we all said our good-byes. Many pictures were taken, and Duncan and Mama Pamela had gifts to give out. I was given three gifts. The first one, they stated, was for my wife, Chris. It was a set of heavy stone coasters with pictures of various African animals on them. Next was a family gift, a plate with two elephants on it and the saying "Nothing can separate us." Last was a gift they said I should put up in my classroom. It was a piece of stone in the shape of the country of Kenya, with an elephant on it. I did not expect the gifts; after all, I was there to give to them. It was a terrific touch from a very classy family. The gifts will always have a very special place in my home.

Then we began the journey, and I do mean journey, back to Nairobi. The plan was to go to Ranen to catch a bus—not a matatu, but a real bus. It was my understanding that it would go directly to Nairobi without any stops. At 11:30, we had no bus. About twenty minutes later, a bus went speeding by us and did not stop. George, who was taking us back to Nairobi, went to ask the guy in charge what happened. We learned that the bus was full, so it did not stop. We sat back down and waited. We were told that the next bus would arrive at 12:30. I thought, *Not too bad.* The 12:30 bus became the 1:45 bus, but we were finally on our way to Nairobi—but it wasn't nonstop. We made many stops in many villages along the way.

The bus was totally full, and two different women on the bus had a chicken. Yes, a live chicken. I had been hoping we would enter the Nairobi area during the daytime, when it would be easier to deal with the craziness of driving there. However, when it turned dark we were just entering the outskirts of the large city. We did not get to where the bus left us, in the heart of Nairobi, until 8:30 p.m. So we got off the bus, grabbed our luggage, and walked to where we were to meet the driver who would take us to Wendy and Cindy's home. We met the young man who was to be our driver; however, there was a problem: he did not own the car we were to take, and he could not find the man who owned it to get the keys. Thus we were in the middle of a lot of craziness, in not the greatest area of Nairobi, and we were stuck. We talked about our options, and eventually George was able to get us another driver who ended up taking us just about a mile down the road, where we stopped and met up with Wendy. Then we headed back to her home.

Wendy and Cindy proceeded to make us an outstanding dinner. After a very long and hectic day, it was nice to relax and have a nice meal. I then washed up and went to bed for my last night in Kenya.

Wednesday, August 12, 2009

Since I did not fly out till 11:45 p.m., I spent the day relaxing at Wendy and Cindy's home. I had learned that the power situation had gotten worse since my first stay there; the power would go off in the morning sometime between 6:00 and 7:00 a.m. and not come back on until about 6:00 p.m. I woke up about 6:45 a.m. and realized that I'd better get myself in the shower quickly, before the power went out, because in this shower, as soon as the power went out, the water went cold. I got in the shower and got the water to a nice temperature and washed my body. Then I lathered up my hair with shampoo and the power went out. Here I was in the dark, with soapy hair and ice-cold water. I used the cold water to get the shampoo out of my hair as well as I could. Then I carefully dried off in the dark, got dressed, and worked my way back to my bedroom.

I spent most of the day finishing *Three Cups of Tea*, an excellent book that I highly recommend. At 8:30 p.m., my ride came to take me to the airport. We made our way through the crazy Nairobi traffic and I was dropped off at the Kenya Airlines ("The Pride of Africa") door. Inside the terminal, I had to wait in a very long line to get my boarding pass. Many of the people in line were high school and college groups from the United Kingdom and the United States who were in Kenya on mission trips. It took about forty-five minutes to go through what would be the first layer of security and get my boarding pass.

I sat and read some more before eventually learning that I needed to go through another level of security to get to the gate. At 11:45 p.m., we were on our way to London. I arrived at Terminal 4 a bit after 6:00 a.m. London time and made my way via bus to Terminal 1, where I could get my United flight back to Chicago. I had to wait until my flight at 11:20 a.m., and so I walked around, got something to eat, and did some more reading. I tried to get some sleep (I cannot sleep on a plane) but was not able to.

My fight landed in Chicago, and customs went very quickly. My luggage was right on the ramp, and so I called the limo for the ride home.

How could I even begin to summarize this unbelievable journey I had taken? It was really overwhelming to even try to begin.

First, I wondered what my relationship with Dago would be in the future. Clearly I wanted to keep that relationship and do some things to help out. The problem was, the needs were so overwhelming. They needed everything. As I returned to my life and let it all sink in, I would have to put this into perspective and decide how I could best help within the limitations of my own resources. I knew it could be very easy to just get back to my busy life and forget about the people of Dago.

The Kenyan people were incredibly kind, polite, courteous, and hospitable. They could not have done more to make me feel welcome and comfortable. At times it was almost too much, how they went out of their way to make me feel welcome. And I do not just mean Duncan, Mama Pamela, and their family—it was pretty much everyone I met in Kenya, and that was a lot of people. It was incredible how, everywhere I went, people would come up to me to say, "Welcome to Kenya," or, "How do you like Kenya?" They all seemed so genuine when they talked to me.

I did not want to come across as a person who had spent two weeks in Kenya and now considered myself an expert on the country. I was certainly no expert, but I did feel an obligation to share my experiences, and the readers or listeners could take it for whatever they wanted.

The vast majority of Kenyans lived in incredibly poor conditions. Their poverty made poverty in the United States seem almost like middle-class living. Corruption was a major problem, from the police to basic services. It was a very sensitive issue for everyone and would take a strong effort on the part of the government to fix it. President Obama and Secretary of State Hillary Clinton had both made it very clear to Kenya's leaders that they had to address this matter quickly and with fervor. Other major problems were things like unsafe water and a road system that made it difficult and dangerous for citizens and commerce to move around the country. Crime in the capital city was clearly another major problem. The economics teacher in me knew that they had to do a better job of managing their economy to expand the Gross Domestic Product and give the people a chance to improve their lives. For years, their GDP growth had been very limited, and now inflation was a major problem. Poverty had been getting worse, and so their economic problems were incredibly difficult.

Education was of course another major problem. It was clear that there were still many children who either never went to school or had a very limited education, with only a few years of primary school. Most children who went to school did so under conditions even the poorest of children in the United States did not have to face. They went to schools where the facilities were poor, supplies and other resources were limited, and overall learning conditions were completely insufficient. Since we all knew that education was the key to success, major efforts needed to be made in order to improve education. They seemed to be making some progress, but very slowly.

All in all, I was glad I finally had the courage to make the trip. What would the future bring? Only time would tell.

> If you have a dream, you can spend a lifetime
> studying, planning, and getting ready for it. What
> you should be doing is getting started.
> —Drew Houston

How the Bernard and Elsie Weiss Dago Scholarship Fund Got Started

After my education I will spearhead corruption
which is the basics of our problems.
The physically and mentally challenged and the illiterate
and semi–illiterate will be helped under my care.
—Boss, scholarship recipient

In the summer of 2010, I began to have thoughts of doing something more substantial to help the children of Dago, Kenya. By this time, my students and I had spent a semester raising money to buy one hundred new pairs of shoes for the children and another semester raising money to buy backpacks and new uniforms for many of the children. The next year we would take on other projects, like raising money to buy Duncan two new cows when we learned that one of his cows had died. It was a great opportunity for my students to learn how important a cow is to a community like Dago. We also bought thirty new water filters that would be scattered around the school and orphanage in Dago so the children had safe water to drink. This was another great opportunity for my students to learn another valuable lesson, how the lack of access to safe water was a major problem in villages like Dago. This was a major cause of death in these kinds of villages. Whenever I talked about these topics with my students, I always tried to make the point that we had to realize how lucky and blessed we were to live the lives we did. Any one of us could have been born in a village like Dago.

But I kept coming back to the idea that while all these needs were critical (let's face it, they needed pretty much everything), there were solutions that did more to change things for the long run in this kind of village. As an educator and someone who was passionate about the importance of education, I kept thinking about how the average person in Kenya had only four years of schooling. In villages like Dago, most of the adults had less than that, and for years, only a handful of people had ever gone to high school. Only about 20 percent of all children in Kenya went to high school, and most of them went because someone was sponsoring them. Most of the children did not even make it to seventh or eighth grade, especially the girls. I kept thinking, *How in the world do we ever begin to change this vicious cycle of poverty, from one generation to another, unless we address education?*

The key reason most children did not go to high school was because the government, which paid for most but not all of a child's primary school education, did not really pay for a high school education. The high schools were boarding schools, and school fees, uniforms, books, and other costs had to be paid for by the family. The overwhelming majority of families in Kenya could not even come close to paying this kind of money.

At this time I was already sponsoring Victor, whom I had met on my first trip in 2009. I was sending him to a private school called St. Benedict for seventh and eighth grades. I was doing this because in Kenya, just like in my world, there were private and public schools, but in Kenya the quality difference between them was huge. The Dago Kogelo Primary School was public and just did not have the resources private schools had, because it was dependent on government money. Private schools went out and raised money from people around the world to get their resources. Looking back, one of the best decisions I ever made was sending Victor to this private school, because he really flourished and grew there.

So I started thinking more and more about starting a scholarship fund to help children from Dago go to high school. I remember that one of the first thoughts that went through my head was, *How in the world am I going to do this?* Kenya was eight thousand miles away, and (at least at that time) I had no way of directly communicating with the people there. I knew very little about their education system and how I would work out all the logistics to make something like this happen. How would I decide which students we would support? And then there was also the issue of fundraising. How would I actually raise the money to do this?

Then of course there was the issue of whether I should create my own nonprofit or just "piggyback" on another one and use its nonprofit status as my own. And then how would I know how these students were doing? Would I be able to keep in touch with them? Would I need to go visit them while they were in high school? The questions were many, and the more I thought, the more questions I had. It began to feel as though it would just be too much.

So I started writing down a lot of my thoughts and asking people about my ideas to see what thoughts they had. A key event was when I learned about the documentary *A Small Act*, which came out in 2010. Someone had told me about it and asked if I had seen it. When I said I had not, he told me that it was a must-see for me. So I went out and bought the documentary and watched it, and then I understood why I'd been told to watch it. I do not want to spoil the documentary for anyone, so I will not mention the details. However it centers on a man named Chris Mburu, who grew up in a small Kenyan village similar to Dago. I loved the documentary, and it did two main things for me:

1. It taught me a lot about how to set up a scholarship fund for high school students in Kenya and what some of the challenges are.
2. It gave me what I call the "kick in the butt"—the motivation to just go out and do it.

Thus I created the Bernard and Elsie Weiss Dago Scholarship Fund. Bernard and Elsie were my mom and dad, who had passed away within a few months of each other a few years earlier. Both of them grew up very poor in different parts of Chicago and were Depression babies. Neither of them was able to go to college, but they really made getting an education very important in our family. They worked hard to make sure their children had the opportunity to get a college degree. I decided one of the best things I could do to honor the memory of my parents was to name this scholarship after them.

I was planning my second trip to Kenya for the summer of 2011. I would go over my plans with the people in Dago to get things started. The school year in Kenya was the calendar year, with students going to school much of the year. Before I watched *A Small Act*, I knew a bit about an exam called the Kenyan Certificate of Primary Education (KCPE) but the documentary greatly increased my understanding of it. At the end of class eight, all students took this exam. This was the big exam in Kenya and what determined who went to high school and which high school they would go to. This would become my main tool for deciding who got a scholarship. While personally I have major issues with standardized tests in the United States, in Kenya I really had no other way to decide which students I should choose.

Then I had to think about being a nonprofit. I decided I did not want to really become my own nonprofit because of the costs involved and the necessity of hiring an accountant and a lawyer. Village Volunteers, the sensational organization I had chosen to partner with on my first trip, could become the organization I piggy-backed onto in order to get the advantages of nonprofit status. I had a number of conversations with Shana Greene, the founder and director of Village Volunteers, to arrange this. So my scholarship fund would become part of Village Volunteers. This meant that we would be able to use its nonprofit status to get the benefits of being a nonprofit. There were other benefits also. Village Volunteers would handle the logistics of accepting the donations, sending people e-mails for their tax donations, managing the money, and wiring the money to Kenya when we needed to pay fees to the various high schools. I would get all these services for only 5 percent of the donations. Today that is a great bargain for me, as I do not think it really even covers their costs, between charge card fees, wiring fees to Kenya, administrative costs, and so forth. I have actually told Shana over the years that she probably should charge more. Shana provides the same kind of service for a number of projects like mine.

Next I needed to create a scholarship application form for the students and establish the rules of the fund. Shana sent me a copy of an application she'd used for a similar program. I modeled my application form largely after that one. On the first page I would ask the students for basic personal information, like their name, information about their parents or guardians and their siblings, their KCPE score, and so forth. (The KCPE exam was worth a total of five hundred points, with five one-hundred-point sections on various subjects.) Then I would have the children write a short essay on questions like "What has life been like for you growing up?" "Why do you want this scholarship?" "What do you want to be when you grow up?" and "How will you give back to the village of Dago after you have received your education?"

As I was creating all of this, I was not even sure how the people in Dago would get me the completed applications. I knew that since I was going back in 2011, I could just bring them the applications for this first year. It turned out that the way they got the scholarship applications back to me was that Mama Pamela took a matatu to a larger city where there was a man whose business had electricity and a computer, e-mail access, and a printer-scanner. It cost a lot of money to make it happen, but it was the only way to get it done.

Next I had to create what the rules would be for the fund. There were two key issues that I had learned a lot about from my first trip, but that the documentary *A Small Act* strongly reinforced in my mind. I'd learned that in poor countries there were many cases where a student got a scholarship to go to high school but then, after a year or two, were told that the money had run out and there was no more scholarship. This hit me pretty hard, and so I decided I never wanted to be in that situation. Thus I made a rule that when we told a child we would sponsor him or her, this meant we had enough money in the bank to pay for all four years. I decided I never wanted to have to tell a child, "Sorry, but we can no longer sponsor you," because if I did it would mean the end of his or her high school education.

In making this decision, I fully realized that this would limit how many children we could sponsor right away. In the first year, I had to budget $3,000 for four years of high school, or $750 per year. On a side note, think about all we were getting for this money—four years of education, room and board, school fees, books, tuition, and uniforms. That is stunning when you compare what that kind of money would get you in the United States. In the first year, January 2012, I raised about $6,000. This meant I committed to two students for four years. If I had wanted to only commit to a year, I could have sponsored eight students; however, then I would have had to scramble every year after that to raise enough money to keep all our current students in high school. By this time I had learned that that was how a number of nonprofits handled this issue, but scrambling for money each year became a big problem for them. I wanted to make sure I avoided that at all costs, even if it meant sponsoring fewer students up front.

The next big issue to address was the gender issue. I had certainly learned in my first trip that in Dago, life was much tougher for girls than for boys. There were still a lot of old-fashioned ideas in Dago that girls did not need an education, that they should just learn how to cook and take care of a home. Whenever there was a problem where a family needed a child to stay home and help out, they would ask only girls, never boys. And when girls were old enough to have their periods, quite often they had to stay home as a hygiene issue. So girls tended to miss a lot of school days, and as a result, most girls quit school at a very young age. Even the girls who tried to battle this trend tended to fall behind in school because they would end up missing a lot more days than the boys did. So at some point many of them fell so far behind that they just gave up and quit. This is why, by the time they were in class eight, there were far fewer girls left than boys.

Then when they got to the KCPE exam, the boys tended to score a lot higher than the girls. So for a small scholarship fund like mine, if we gave out scholarships based only on KCPE scores, the girls might never get a scholarship. This did not mean that girls were not as smart as boys; it simply meant that they had far more challenges and roadblocks in life. This had to be addressed, and it was a key issue that was dealt with very directly in *A Small Act*. We know that if a girl gets a chance at a high school education, she can do just as well, if not better, than a boy, but she has to get the chance. I get uncomfortable even saying that, because of course I wish I could create a scenario where all these children got scholarships and we would not have to choose. However I did not have the power or the money to do that, so we had to make these tough choices. We also knew that, in reality, there are far more benefits to society when girls get an education, compared to boys.

Here is some data published in 2013 by the United Nations Educational, Scientific and Cultural Organization, highlighting the benefits of educating girls in very poor countries:

1. Education reforms increased education attainment among young women by 1.8 years in Kenya, accounting for a 34 percent decline in maternal mortality.
2. In low-income countries, mothers who have completed primary school are 12 percent more likely than mothers with no education to seek appropriate health care when their child has diarrhea.
3. If all women had a secondary education, there would be 49 percent fewer child deaths
4. In the United Republic of Tanzania, children aged six months to twenty-three months whose mothers had at least a secondary education were almost twice as likely to consume

food rich in micronutrients as children whose mothers had less than a primary education.

5. In Ethiopia, 32 percent of girls with less than a primary education were married before the age of fifteen, compared with fewer than 9 percent of those with secondary education.

6. If education inequality in sub-Saharan Africa had been halved to the level of Latin America and the Caribbean, the annual per-capita growth rate from 2005 to 2010 would have been 47 percent higher.

7. In Kenya, if women farmers are given the same level of education as their male partners, their yields for maize, beans, and cowpeas increase by up to 22 percent.

8. According to the World Bank, education plays an important role in giving women more control over how many children they have. An extra year of female schooling reduces fertility rates by 10 percent.

9. A child born to a mother who can read is 50 percent more likely to survive past age five.

10. In sub-Saharan Africa, an estimated 1.8 million children's lives could have been saved in 2008 if their mothers had at least a secondary education.

11. Children of educated mothers are more likely to be vaccinated and less likely to be stunted because of malnourishment. In Indonesia, child vaccination rates are 19 percent when mothers have no education. This increases to 68 percent when mothers have at least a secondary school education.

12. According to UNAIDS, women with post primary education are five times more likely than illiterate women to be educated on the topic of HIV and AIDS.

13. Girls with higher levels of education are less likely to get married at an early age. If all girls had a primary education, there would be 14 percent fewer child marriages. If all girls had a secondary education, there would be two-thirds fewer child marriages.

So a key rule became that all money would be divided equally between boys and girls. This had to be a rule, and it had to be firm. I knew this rule would be controversial, and it sure became that. It meant that we would be giving scholarships to girls who had lower KCPE scores than some boys we turned down. In a world where many of the adults, even some women, believe it is not important for a girl to get an education, this would be challenged. During my future trips, I would be questioned by more than one parent whose son was turned down for a scholarship even though he had a better score than a girl who had received a scholarship. I would explain my position, and the parent would politely listen and then end the conversation. I knew these parents were not happy, but I do think in part they understood. And as a parent myself, I fully understood their frustration

When I talked about this with my students, I told them that getting turned down for one of my scholarships was not like applying for college, where if you got turned down by Harvard, you could go to the University of Illinois instead. Not getting to go to high school, to quote Chris Mburu from *A Small Act*, was really a matter of life and death in Kenya. When children did not get to go to high school, it was highly probable that their lives would not be much different than their parents'. They would live in mud huts with no electricity or plumbing, make a dollar or two a day when they could find work, and never be quite sure where their next meal was coming from, and they might never see a doctor. And in the case of girls, they would quickly be married off and start having babies. The vicious cycle of extreme poverty would just continue. I have said many, many times that the hardest part of this scholarship fund is thinking about all the students who do not get chosen. There are times when that has been really hard for me to deal with, so I have to learn to just focus on the good we are doing with the students we do choose.

Another issue to deal with was the criteria for how we would decide which students to choose. Should it be just the KCPE score, or should we take other factors into consideration? Mama Pamela and Duncan wanted us to include in the rules that choices would be based on KCPE scores and need. My first thought about that was, *Isn't everyone in Dago needy?* They told me that there could be a situation where a child we chose came from a family with the ability to pay for high school on their own, and in that case we would not give that child a scholarship. They wanted to leave it open as a possibility. As of this writing, this has never happened.

Chris Mburu says in his documentary, "I know I cannot relieve all of the pain and suffering in the world. However, I want to do one thing to make this world a better place." Doing that one thing is much better than doing nothing. This is why I have told people, including my students, over and over that they should never feel they can't help out when there's a problem. Any help, no matter how small, makes a situation better and the world a better place.

So now I had my key rules, and I developed an application. I sent my first draft of the application to Patrick Odoyo (one of Mama Pamela and Duncan's sons, who now was living in Evansville, Indiana) for him to review. His first comment was something I should have realized: I'd written the application in American English, and it needed to be in British English, because that's what people in Kenya speak and write. So I had to make changes in the application so the students reading it would know what each word meant. I prepared a number of copies of the application and a separate sheet with the rules to take with me to Kenya on my second trip in the summer of 2011. I would use this time to spread the word about the scholarship and encourage all the class eight students to work hard in order to make the highest score possible on the KCPE. I told them that I would be able to award scholarships based on the amount of money I raised. Of course, at that time I had no idea how much I would be able to raise.

When the end of the year came, I was anxious to get the KCPE results and applications from the students. We decided we would ask the top five boys and top five girls to complete applications. Then, based on the money we'd raised, we'd decide how many children we could help and then which ones we would award the scholarship to. The Bernard and Elsie Weiss Dago Scholarship Fund was becoming a reality!

Education is the most powerful weapon which
you can use to change the world.
—Nelson Mandela

If we want to reach real peace in this world,
we should start educating the children.
—Mahatma Gandhi

Kenya 2011 Trip

> My dream is to become a lecturer. I pray to God to help
> me become a lecturer in colleges and universities.
> I will be the song of our community and many
> people will succeed through me.
> —Mercy, scholarship recipient

Getting out of Chicago for this trip ended up being way too complicated. I arrived at O'Hare around noon to catch a flight to New York to start the journey. (I will leave the name of the airline out of this for reasons that will become obvious.) I went to check in and was told that the flight I was booked on no longer existed. Of course I was, to say the least, shocked. I showed the agent my paperwork and said there must be a mistake. He checked again but said there was no mistake. I started to get nervous and a bit angry. He told me that I'd received an e-mail about a month earlier telling me that the flight had been removed from their schedule. I told him that I was very diligent about checking my e-mail and I never received such an e-mail. He insisted that I did, and then he checked some more on his computer. All of a sudden his jaw kind of dropped, and he looked at me and told me I was right: they never sent me an e-mail.

I had four pieces of luggage with me and needed to be on a flight that left New York at 7:30 p.m. for London. I tried to stay calm and asked him what I should do. After being a bit cold to me at first, he began to have some sympathy for me. He started to look at options that could get me to New York in time. After about fifteen minutes, he had a plan for me. There was a flight leaving right away for Cincinnati. Of course I said I did not want to go to Cincinnati; I needed to get to New York. He told me that once I landed in Cincinnati, there was a flight to New York that would get me there in time.

I agreed and paid for the new tickets. I brought up the idea of getting my money back, but he said he could not do that. (In the end, although I complained a lot, I never did get a refund.) The flight I needed to get on was one terminal over, and I had very little time and four pieces of luggage. He gave me a cart I could use to put my luggage on, and I started to move very quickly to catch my new flight. I arrived at the gate, checked in, and boarded the plane. I was quite out of breath but happy to be on the plane.

When I arrived in Cincinnati, I called my wife, because I hadn't had time to call her with the craziness I'd gone through at O'Hare. My wife always has a copy of my agenda when I travel. When she answered the phone, I said, "Hi from Cincinnati!" Of course she said, "What are you doing in Cincinnati?" I had to explain everything that had happened back in Chicago, but I did not have a lot of time because I had to board my plane to New York. After explaining, I said good-bye, telling her I would call her next from London. One of my worries now was about my luggage, because on my last trip one of my suitcases hadn't made it on time.

I was very excited about this trip. I would be spending some time first at a private school in Maasai country and then I'd go to Dago. I had done some reading about the Maasai people, and they seemed very unique; I was looking forward to learning more about them firsthand. In Dago, my main task was to officially announce the start of the Bernard and Elsie Weiss Dago Scholarship Fund. I was bringing the applications for the students to fill out and needed to work out the logistics for how everything would happen. On my first trip, I'd had no idea what to expect, but with this trip, I had many things I wanted to accomplish.

Thursday, July 7, 2011

Finally I was safe and sound at Wendy's home in Nairobi. One of my checked bags made it, but the other bag with some of my stuff, T-shirts for the children, and various gifts I was bringing, such as school supplies, did not make it. I was told the bag would arrive tomorrow, but first thing in the morning I was headed to Maasai country to meet Emmanuel, who ran a private primary school. Wendy served us a great dinner, and I headed to bed.

Friday, July 8, 2001

After I had a nice shower in the morning, we headed out through Nairobi for Maasai country. It was a bit longer drive than the one to Dago, so it would take the better part of the day. I was thrilled to be back in Kenya, and one of the things that hit me once again was how in Kenya they drove on the left side of the road and the steering wheel was on the right. It was always hard to get used to that. Also, I'd been told there had been big improvements in the road system, but I was really not seeing that.

About 3:00 p.m., we arrived in the town of Kilgoris and I met Emmanuel. I had heard a lot about him over the past two years, so it was really a pleasure to meet him. He bought lunch at a place called the Shalom Restaurant, and then we headed to his home. The drive took about thirty-five minutes on an extremely bumpy dirt road. When I mentioned how bad the road was, Emmanuel told me that the road was actually much better than it used to be. Later I would learn that the government and the Maasai people did not get along very well, and it seemed that one of the ways the government punished them was to do less for their roads than for other roads in Kenya.

When we arrived at his home, I was led to the hut where I would be staying. It was made of concrete and had a thatched roof. There were two bunk beds in this hut, and there was an identical hut next to it. Right now I was the only volunteer there, so I got the hut to myself. I needed to go to the bathroom, so I asked Emmanuel where it was. I learned that this bathroom was much more primitive than the one in Dago. It was simply a room with a concrete floor and a hole in the center of it. I was not thrilled, but I told myself I could survive anything for a few days.

I walked around the grounds a bit, taking pictures. Emmanuel and his wife, Lillian, were building a new home, and it was almost done, but they still lived in the old one. From the outside, the new home looked gorgeous. Then Emmanuel and I sat down on a couple of chairs outside and just started to talk. This reminded me so much of being in Dago two years earlier, when there were many times I wanted to be recording everything I was hearing, but that would have been rude. For about two hours we talked about all kinds of things, and it was fascinating. Emmanuel had a degree in library science and was very knowledgeable about education and world events. He was clearly well read.

We talked a bit about how the Maasai people had faced a lot of discrimination compared to other tribes in Kenya. Up until recently, the Maasai had been nomads, moving to different areas during the different times of the year. Historically, education was not stressed in Maasai families. Several years earlier, the government of Kenya had begun putting a lot of pressure on the Maasai to stop being nomads and settle in one place. So now most Maasai were not nomads, but they were not happy with their lives. They were being forced to be farmers but really knew little about farming.

Emmanuel told me the other tribes had always looked down on the Maasai, saying that they were not very bright and refused to keep up with modern changes. I learned that this was a big part of what drove Emmanuel and why he started his school to help Maasai children get an education.

Emmanuel's own story was fascinating. His father had four wives (not all that uncommon for Kenyan men of that age) and his mother was very serious about education. She had wanted badly to get an education, but because of discrimination against girls, she was never able to get one. However, she instilled the importance of an education in Emmanuel, although he did not even start school until he was nine years old. When I asked how he paid for high school, he talked about how from time to time when he was little, he would buy a goat, until finally he had many goats. He would pay for his high school expenses by selling his goats. He wanted to go to college and was accepted, but he did not have the money. He talked about doing a number of different things to make the money, even becoming the minister of a church despite the fact that he was not a minister. He got married and had two children right away, and he did not start college until after they were born. He talked quite a bit about how he, Lillian, and the two children lived in the slums of Nairobi while he worked as a clerk for the government. He said that five-year period was the worst time of his life. I had seen the slums of Nairobi, and they were far, far worse than anything we would call a slum in the United States.

To go to college, he literally went out and did fundraising. He kept raising money until he had his college degree. This was clearly a man who understood the importance of an education and was really determined to get one. His story was very inspiring.

He next talked about how he'd started his school three years earlier. He currently had about 275 students through class seven, so next year would be the first time he would have class eight students. Half his students were boarders, and the others walked to school each day. He had students from as far away as Nairobi. He welcomed students from all tribes, but 90 percent of his were Maasai. His school was private and thus not a part of the public school system; it was funded from tuition that parents paid and from donations. He mentioned that they worked with each family to allow them to pay whatever they could afford. Some families paid with things like cows, goats, and milk.

Emmanuel was clearly passionate about his school and wanted to have five of them in the area eventually. He was extremely well organized and seemed to have a real vision for where he wanted to take his ideas. This all led me to bring up the documentary *A Small*

Act to see if he knew about it. He knew a little bit about it, as he'd recently had a Jewish family from California stay at the school, and they'd told him they were inspired to do volunteer work from the documentary. I gave him an overview of the story.

It started getting dark and then it started to rain, which forced me to move into my hut. Emmanuel had solar power through all the schools and other buildings on his compound, so I had a nice electric bulb giving me some decent light. We would be eating dinner in a bit, and then we were getting up at 4:45 a.m., as Emmanuel was taking me on a safari. Part of the money I'd paid for this trip went to Emmanuel and his school for this safari. After my first trip, many of my friends were shocked that I had not gone on a safari. To be frank, going on a safari was not a high priority for me, plus I knew that you had to pay the safari companies a lot of money for their services. When I found out that I could go on a safari with Emmanuel for a lot less money, and that all the money would go to his school, I jumped on it. We were going on a safari at Maasai Mara. He told me that on Saturday I would learn a great deal about his school, as we would visit it. The school was about a mile from his home, and I was really looking forward to seeing it. I had seen pictures on the Internet, but I needed to see it in person.

There was so much to learn. I was already feeling a bit overwhelmed, as almost every minute I was bombarded with things that were new to me. It was a lot to take in, but fascinating. There were so many ways to live this thing we call life. These folks could learn a lot from us, but we could learn a lot, maybe even more, from them. They were always working incredibly hard.

For dinner we had beef, pasta, and spinach, and it was very good. I learned that I would have a lot more beef here than in Dago, because cows were such an important part of life here. I ate with Emmanuel, Lillian, and their two daughters. Lillian was very quiet, and I was wondering if she spoke English, but the next night I learned she spoke it very well.

Emmanuel shared a story. I had noticed when I met him earlier that day that his two front lower teeth were missing. He told me that in the Maasai tradition, when a boy got to be ten years old they pulled out those teeth. He explained that there were medical reasons initially, but now it was just a tradition for boys. He said it was kind of a welcome to manhood to see if the boy could take the pain. If he passed, he get a cow, which was a really big deal here. I learned that cows were very special and important to the Maasai. He said it was also done to see if the boy could handle circumcision, which happened at about the age of fifteen. I had never heard of a circumcision that late in life. I then learned that because of medical advances and education, most Maasai no longer took out the two front teeth. However, the circumcision ritual remained the same.

At 10:00 p.m., I returned to my hut from dinner. I wanted to get to bed right away, as we had an early start in the morning. I was hoping my bag would be there when I got back from the safari.

July 8, 2011

I got up at 4:00 a.m. and began getting ready to leave for the safari at 5:00 a.m. I was wondering what kind of remarkable moments were in store for me that day. What new things would I learn? A lot of this trip for me was about pushing myself to do things that I never thought I would do or that I was just afraid of doing. Each time I reach that moment, I always find I can do it. It is amazing the kind of things we humans can do when we just put our minds to it and are determined. I used the bathroom, and while it was not what I would call pleasant, it all was fine. It was just another in a long list of new experiences. I was excited to spend an entire day one-on-one with Emmanuel. He was a brilliant man and a very deep thinker. I learned something new every time he spoke.

By 10:00 p.m. I was back in my hut after a fascinating day. We left just after 5:00 a.m. to drive on very bumpy dirt roads to Maasai Mara to see the animals. One of the most exciting moments of the day was when I got within about twenty feet of two lions. I was told that you could go a whole day without ever seeing one, but here were two right in front of me. I saw so many animals during the day, many of which I had never even heard of and whose names I probably will never remember. However, these two lions I will never forget. We were riding in Emmanuel's SUV, and when we saw the lions, we pulled up so that they were about twenty feet from my side of the vehicle. I rolled down the window and starting taking pictures of the lions, which were just relaxing under a tree. All of a sudden I started thinking that if these two lions decided to jump toward me, I could be in trouble. I asked Emmanuel about this. He could be quite funny when he wanted to be. He said, "I can tell they have recently just eaten, so you are okay."

I had never experienced anything like this, and it was truly amazing. I saw all these animals in their natural habitat, not behind bars or glass, and I am not sure why, but I was never afraid. Now I could understand why so many people over the last two years had yelled at me for going to Africa and not going on a safari.

Emmanuel took me to lunch at a lodge called Maasai Serena, which was part of a British company, in the middle of Maasai Mara. It was a gorgeous lodge that looked like it could have been in any Western country. We had a buffet that would rival anything in the United States, from a very complete salad bar to a pasta bar and all kinds of pork, chicken, seafood, and so forth. There was also a stunning dessert table that I could not pass up. I then bought several items from the gift shop. I never thought I would be in a place like this in Kenya. In the gift shop, I had one of those small world moments: I was wearing a T-shirt from my high school, and a young woman came up to me and asked me if I taught there. I told her I did, and it turned out that she lived in an apartment building in Chicago just upstairs from one of my fellow teachers. Small world!

Next I had an incredible experience. I went to a very small Maasai village that comprised three men with all their wives and children. Joseph, the village elder, gave me a complete tour of the village. He explained a lot about Maasai history and how, in this village, the Maasai generally still lived strictly according to their cultural traditions. He did recognize that the world was changing, and he said he understood that men should have "less" wives today. (He had a little smile as he said that.) I had been told the Maasai people were not very comfortable having people take pictures of them, and so I asked him if I could take some pictures. He smiled and handed my camera to Emmanuel, telling him to take pictures as he and I walked around.

A lot of what he talked about was the importance of cows in their culture and how the villagers could not live without them. He encouraged me to ask questions, and I asked plenty. All the adults in the village, and some of the children, wore traditional Maasai robes with their many colors. He explained that the two most important colors to them were red, a symbol of cow's blood, and blue, a symbol of the sky, where God is. Many people I have met in villages like this one know very little about the world outside their community, but Joseph impressed me, as he knew quite a bit about world events. He asked the women of the village to sing a welcome song to me. Finally, after we'd talked for about ninety minutes, he took me to an area where the women sold things they'd made. I definitely wanted to purchase something as a thank you for all his time. I purchased a "peace walking stick," used by a leader to start a meeting so the meeting would be one of peace. It was a beautiful piece of wood about a foot and a half long, with a rounded top. It was decorated with beads of various colors. This would be a beautiful addition to my classroom.

When I returned to Emmanuel's compound, my blue bag was in. Wendy had had it transported from her home to the town of Kilgoris (where Emmanuel picked me up when I arrived), so we drove over there to get up. I finally had all my things. Most of what I had in this bag were gifts, so I made my first gift presentation to Emmanuel and Lillian, a gorgeous picture book of the history of Chicago. This led to an entire conversation about the city, and I talked about all the great things Chicago had to offer. This led to a lot of questions. I learned from Emmanuel that the famous lions in front of the Chicago Art Institute are actually from Kenya. They are among many things England stole from Kenya as they were giving Kenya its independence in 1963, and then England gave many of these things, including the lions, to the United States as gifts. He mentioned that the Kenyan government had been trying for years to get the lions and other stolen things back, but with no success.

It was a great day, and the next day, my last full day here, I would get to visit Emmanuel's school and meet the teachers and students. My time was just way too short here, but we just could not work it out any other way.

July 9, 2011

I spent most of the day at Emmanuel's primary school, Sirua Aulo Academy. He had done an incredible job over the past three years getting this school up and running. It was a private school (as opposed to the Dago Kogelo Primary School, which was public), and it had about 275 students, about half of them boarders. There were separate boys' and girls' dorms. At the moment he had students through class seven, but the next year the school would go through class eight. His students went go to school an incredible number of hours each day and week. The boarders went Monday through Friday from 5:00 a.m. until 9:00 p.m. with breaks, and on Saturday from 8:00 a.m. until 3:00 p.m. The nonboarders went Monday through Saturday from 9:00 a.m. until 4:00 p.m. They all worked incredibly hard. I sat in on a number of classes and took a lot of pictures and videos. Emmanuel really knew a lot about education and how to run a school, and I could see the result in what was going on there. Compared to other schools I had seen in Kenya, his classrooms were much nicer and the teachers had a lot more books and other resources. There seemed to be a real educational plan here that the staff worked hard to implement.

His vision was exciting and quite challenging. From having gotten to know Emmanuel over the past few days, I had a feeling he could make it all happen. In addition to being a great educator, he had a real entrepreneurial spirit and a great knack for marketing.

Emmanuel asked me to meet with the teachers for about an hour, and it ended up being about ninety minutes. He asked me to give them advice on teaching and answer their questions. We had a very interesting session. Their questions were really not any different than the ones teachers in the United States would ask about handling lessons, discipline issues, and so forth. They also talked a lot about typical concerns like needing smaller class sizes and more money for resources and salaries.

At 3:00 p.m., when they stopped school for the day, all the children went down to the river for the weekly washing of their clothes and their bodies. Boys and girls went to separate areas, so I went down to the river with the boys. It was a long trek down the hill, and it gave me an opportunity to have some great discussions with the boys and for them to ask me a lot of questions. At about 4:30, I started the long trek up the hill. It was quite a climb. Emmanuel hired a motorbike to take me back to his home from the school (about a mile), as he had other business to take care of that afternoon.

The plan was for me to go back to the school early the next morning, just for a while, and then Emmanuel would take me to a place where I could meet up with Edwin (Mama Pamela and Duncan's oldest son) to get back to Dago.

I'd been thinking a lot about how similar yet how different my experience with the Maasai had been compared to my visit with the Luo in Dago two years earlier. I knew I should not really compare, but it was hard not to. The obvious similarity was that almost all the people suffered from extreme poverty beyond anything we in the United States can comprehend. The Maasai seemed to have a lot more challenges and had been the brunt of so much discrimination from other tribes in Kenya. There are many analogies I can make between how the Maasai have been treated in Kenya and how Native Americans have been treated in the United States. The Maasai customs are very different, and they seem to have a lot more people fighting the changes that need to be made to improve their livelihood. Emmanuel told me that traditionally the Maasai do not send their children to school, but he had worked very hard to convince lots of parents that education is the only way for their children to have better lives. Given these challenges, I found it even more incredible that Emmanuel had been able to accomplish so much with his school.

The Maasai traditionally are not farmers, but they seemed to be gradually realizing that they needed to do more with farming. Emmanuel told me that the people who were starting to get into farming would hire people from other tribes to do the work, and teach them how to farm. The nomadic days seemed to be ending as the Maasai settled down to be farmers.

In some ways, the past few days had been very hard. I had grown close to Dago over the past couple of years, and now I'd come here and met the Maasai, whose challenges were also great. When I thought about the thousands of villages on this planet that were just as poor, it was an overwhelming feeling. I wanted to dramatically help the lives of each of these children, and knowing that I could not relieve all the suffering was quite painful. I constantly had to remind myself that I could only do what I could do, and nothing more.

July 10, 2011

At 7:00 a.m. Emmanuel took me to Kilgoris, and along with Daniel (the guy he was paying to take care of me), we got on a matatu and headed for Kisii, where we would meet up with Edwin from Dago. I was told the ride would be about an hour. It was two hours—pretty normal for Kenyan time. As always, my ride in the matatu was not for the faint of heart. The vehicle was much more than full, and we stopped at pretty much every village for people to get on and off. The sign on the matatu said it could hold only fourteen passengers, but no one paid attention to that. They easily took double that number. At one point I counted thirty people, and of course that did not take into account all the luggage, bags of grain, and the like, tied to the top and back of the van. It also did not count the animals, such as chickens and goats, that were brought on. Some of the roads were okay, but most were horrible and riddled with potholes. This kind of travel was one of the hardest parts about a journey like this.

We made it to Kisii and met up with Edwin. Then we got on another matatu and headed toward Dago. About ninety minutes later, we got off in Ranen and began the one-mile walk to Mama Pamela and Duncan's home in Dago.

Edwin showed me to my room, and I spent a bit of time unpacking. I wanted to head over to the orphanage as soon as possible. I met Christine, another volunteer from the United States, who was doing some really helpful work with the primary-age children of Dago. She had come with her two teenagers and their two friends. For the next several hours, they led several fun activities they had planned for the children of Dago. Over one hundred children took part. Christine and the teens did a great job with all the children.

It felt like it had been about five minutes since I left Dago two years ago. I had already spent some time talking with Mama Pamela, Duncan, and some of the other adults I met on my previous trip. I had begun my ten days in Dago, and I was looking forward to all that awaited me.

July 11, 2011

I got up at 6:00, had breakfast, and started washing my dirty clothes. Just before 8:00 I saw Christine and the four teens off to begin their journey home. They were going to Nairobi for a couple of days and then back to the United States. Christine had raised money to start a half-day preschool program and had already hired a teacher. Yesterday she met with all the children and parents who would be a part of this program. This was a very impressive and much-needed project. They had no preschool in Dago, and since there was no kindergarten either, the children did not start school until age six, which meant that they were missing a lot of educational opportunities.

After they left, I finished my wash, hung everything up to dry, and then took my tub shower. It was shocking how good even a tub shower could make you feel, even though it was far from a "real" shower. I had not been getting any cell service since I arrived in Dago, and it occurred to me that if that did not change soon, I would need to use someone else's phone to let my wife know I was still alive. In a few minutes I would be going over to the Dago Primary School, which was about a three-minute walk. It looked like tomorrow I would be going to visit Victor (the young man I decided to sponsor from my first visit) at St. Benedict primary school. I was very excited to see him.

I went over and spent some time at the primary school. One of my big goals on this trip was to better understand the structure of the schools, the test scores, and so forth, and I made a good start on that today. It was really important for me to learn all about the schools as we began to put this scholarship program in place. I saw how all the Dago students had scored on the previous year's Kenyan Certificate of Primary Education (KCPE), the test that all class eight students took. I also asked the class seven and eight master teachers (both named Henry) to get me a list of their top ten students over the next few days.

I spent some time with the lady who taught class seven science. She was giving a quiz, and because of the lack of resources, the process was very time-consuming. She wrote ten multiple-choice questions on the blackboard, which was a piece of slate in the mud wall. The children wrote their answers on a piece of paper numbered one through ten. I asked the teacher if I could grade the quizzes, and she said fine. Then it was lunchtime, so I told her I would come back after the children had finished eating.

I got involved in a number of lessons at the school. In class five I went through a math lesson, helping the students convert centimeters, meters, and kilometers. I would put a problem on the board and ask one of the students to come up and work it. We did a number of them, and it went quite well. Next, in class seven, I took part in a lecture and discussion on the Berlin Conference and the Scramble for Africa. The topic is a passion of mine and one of the things that drove me to come to Africa to do what I could to help.

Their teacher did a great job of giving an overview of the topic and involving the students in the discussion. I made the point that this was a topic that most people in the United States knew very little about, which was a shame because it was the start of the European powers doing a lot of horrible things to Africans, using them for slaves or near-slaves and stealing many of their resources, such as gold, silver, zinc, copper, rubber, trees, and so forth. It also divided up Africa among the European powers without the involvement or even the knowledge of the African people. The Europeans did not understand the tribes, nor did they care about them. They created arbitrary boundaries without knowing or caring anything about the tribes' various cultures, histories, religions, or languages. I stressed to the students the importance of learning about this.

I spent more time in the teachers' room, trying to understand how they tested students and learn more about the KCPE exam. I saw reports projecting students' KCPE scores from pretests they had taken. All of this helped me as I prepared for the scholarship fund.

School officially stopped at 4:30 p.m., but as I learned, that rarely meant the end of the school day. The class eight students did the math part of the pretest for the KCPE. Earlier in the day, I had gone through the results with Henry, the class seven math teacher and the school's math expert. We all sat outside, and the students brought their desks out. They had a portable blackboard, and Henry reviewed the problems with them. There were fifty problems, from basic math to algebra and geometry. Many of the questions were quite complex. Henry asked the students which questions they wanted to go over, and for the next two hours they went through about fifteen of them. These students had been at school since 7:30 a.m., yet they were very attentive to the review session.

I walked back to Duncan's home, and he asked me to sit and have some chai. He loved discussing education and current events in Kenya, especially those dealing with politics, and he loved to ask me about the United States. We talked and talked until 8:00 p.m., when it was almost time for dinner to be served. I ran back to my room to grab the two gifts I had for Mama Pamela and Duncan. After dinner

I presented them. The first was a piece of art with the words *peace*, *justice*, and *serenity* on it; I told them this was for all of them and the people of Kenya. The second was the same Chicago picture book I had given Emmanuel and Lillian. Duncan loved looking at the book and immediately asked a lot of questions about Chicago. I was glad I had given them the books, as I wanted to show my appreciation for their great hospitality.

Soon it was time for bed. In the morning, Duncan and I would head off to St. Benedict to visit Victor. I was hoping that somewhere along the way, I could get cell service.

July 12, 2011

It was quite a day. After breakfast, Duncan and I made the one-mile walk down the dirt road to Ranen, where we boarded a matatu to head to Awendo. When we arrived there, I asked Duncan if we could go to a post office, as I had two postcards I wanted to mail. I had stamps on one but needed stamps on the other to get it to the United States. Here is where I began to learn, even more, that everything in Kenya was much more complicated and took longer than it did back home. I am not saying this to complain, but just to pass on information and make the point. We were in the business district of Awendo (a town much larger than Ranen or Dago), where there were a series of shops in some concrete buildings. The shops were tattered and very cramped. At the post office, I tried to find out how many shillings it would take to mail this postcard to the United States, and the conversation became very complicated. At first the clerk said he did not like the size of the postcards I had bought there in Kenya. Eventually that concern went away, and we just had to deal with the cost. I kept saying that I just wanted to make sure the postcard made it to the United States. Eventually we settled on the amount (there did not seem to be any set price), I bought the stamps, he put them on the cards for me, and then I went to put them in the mail slot. It took only about half an hour to get this done.

We then walked to St. Benedict School, which was about a mile away up a large hill. The road up the hill was a dirt road that was very bumpy and full of big potholes and in some ways dangerous. When we arrived at the school, we went to the headmaster's office, where we talked to him and several of the teachers. When I asked to speak to Victor, who was in class seven, I was told that his class was in the middle of an exam, so we had to wait a bit to see him. In the meantime, Duncan found two boys from Dago who were in class eight. They both wanted to be engineers. One young man had delivered a letter to Duncan a few days earlier, saying he needed help paying his fees for high school and then a university. In the letter, he mentioned that he was a "total orphan," which meant that both his parents were dead (probably as a result of AIDS). I was hoping I could get a copy of the letter to take home.

Then I was able to see Victor. He had grown quite a bit in the two years since I first saw him. He was still quite shy and soft-spoken, but we began a very nice conversation after a big hug. I thanked him for the nice letter he'd written me and told him I'd met his mother a couple of days earlier in a meeting at the Dago orphanage. He told me that he wanted to be a broadcaster. I congratulated him on a great report card and told him I would share it with my students.

Then I asked him what things he needed, and he started a long list. He mentioned a number of textbooks, items related to his uniform, and personal toiletry items. I was a bit frustrated with the list, wondering how he could need so many things, especially the books, as the money I'd paid was supposed to cover those. This was another event that helped me learn that things in Kenya were much more complicated than they were in my world. It took a few hours for me to understand it all.

Duncan and I took the list and walked down the hill to a bookstore located in a business area that was very crowded, with all dirt roads and no sidewalks. We were able to buy most of the books we needed there. We went to a second bookstore, which did not have the other books we needed, but we were able to get most of them at a third store. Still, there were a few books we could not find, so I decided that I would leave money with Duncan and hope he could get them at another time.

We then went to a store to get things like toothpaste, toilet paper, and other toiletries. Then it was time to walk back up the hill and get all these things to Victor. We went to see the headmaster, and he was quite happy with what we had bought. Some of it would be needed the next year in class eight and would help him prepare for the KCPE. One thing we did not buy was something Victor called "rubber shoes." I learned that this is what we call a gym shoe, and his were all worn out. I would be leaving money with Duncan for those also. The headmaster had called for Victor, and when he arrived, we went through all the things we had purchased, and he was quite pleased and appreciative. He said he needed to go back to his dorm room to put everything in his "box." I was not quite sure what this meant, but we headed that way.

The dorm was a big room with many bunk beds, sort of like a military barracks. It was pretty crowded, but not bad compared to other places I had seen in Kenya. His "box" was a small footlocker on his bed. There was a lock on it, but Victor told me the lock was broken, and what he meant was that you could reach into his box even when it was locked. Between his box and that of another boy with whom he shared his bunk bed, he put away all the things we bought him.

The current school term ended on July 25, and then the children would go home. I gave the headmaster some money to help Victor pay for the matatu that would get him back home, and for other travels. The students were off for a couple of weeks; however, the school had coaching sessions during the breaks. As I explained earlier, the students were expected to attend these sessions, which gave them help with all their schoolwork, but the sessions cost extra money. I paid the two thousand shillings (about $22) for Victor to attend these sessions. So Victor would be home for about a week and then come back for the coaching. I gave Mama Pamela and Duncan another three thousand shillings (about $33) to buy a new pair of gym shoes and the books we were not able to find. They would then give all of this to Victor when he was home on break.

It had been an outstanding yet very emotional day. It reminded me how challenging life was for people who lived in communities like Dago. But while it was hard for me to watch, for them it was just life. They really did not know how much easier life could be.

During my first trip to Dago, and already several times during my second trip, there were moments when I was alone at night and tears came to my eyes. These were the moments when all of it seemed overwhelming. I'd spent much of this day helping Victor. Sadly, there were millions of Victors all over Africa and the rest of the world. It can be sad when you see this kind of suffering on television or in the movies or read about them in a book, newspaper, or magazine; however, it is much more difficult when you experience it firsthand. You cannot help but wonder, *Why does life have to be so tough for these children, when so many children around the world have much easier lives?* When I go through that thought process, I have to get my mind back to the place where I just tell myself, *I am only one person, and I can only do what I can do. As much as I would like to, I cannot end all the suffering of all the children in the world.*

Today I gave additional support to Victor, and it gave him a big smile. I hope it left him knowing there were many people who cared about him. At the end of the day, I just needed to feel good about that.

Another thought on my mind was how tough these teachers were on their students. I had always felt that it wasn't my place to tell the people of Dago how to live their lives; my mission was to see how I could help them. During my first trip, I once mentioned to one of the teachers I'd gotten to know pretty well how tough I thought he was on the students. I thought his reply was a pretty good one. As I stated earlier, he said something like "Look, Kenya is a very poor country, and these students are very poor. We must be tough on them if they are to have a better life and make Kenya better country." Today, as Victor spent time with Duncan and the headmaster, they said to him over and over that with all the help he was getting from me, his job was to perform. They were mainly referring to the KCPE exam he would take at the end of class eight, which would determine whether he would even go to high school and, if he did, the quality of the high school he would attend. I had seen these kinds of comments made over and over to students like Victor. I worried that we may have been putting way too much pressure on them. In the United States, we worried about the psychological ramifications of putting too much pressure on students. But was it possible that we worried too much? I was just not sure.

One final story about my visit to St. Benedict:

The headmaster and I exchanged e-mails so we could communicate when I was back in the United States. About a month after I returned home, I received an e-mail from him. I was hoping it was an update on how Victor was doing. Instead he gave me a big surprise: he told me he really wanted to get his master's degree and asked if I could pay for it. I chuckled a bit, knowing this was another example of how needy the people of Kenya were. At first I was not pleased that he would ask me for such a favor, but I let it go pretty quickly. I wrote him back letting him know that I was not in a position to help him, but I wished him luck in being able to get this money.

After dinner tonight, I went through everything I'd put together to start my scholarship fund, including the rules and the application. I would be reviewing all of it with the class seven and class eight students and having a meeting with the class eight parents and guardians to explain it all and answer questions. We wanted to make sure they all knew about the process, felt it was fair, and were excited about the opportunity.

July 13, 2011

I was at the Dago Primary School all morning, visiting classes and talking with the teachers. I presented all the teachers with the gifts I'd brought for the school. They included boxes of pens, pencils, two pencil sharpeners, a box of crayons, a small whiteboard with many markers, a children's book about Harriet Tubman, and a children's atlas of the world. They were all like children on Christmas morning. There was so little they had and so much they needed. The young man who was the main social studies teacher just loved the atlas. He would not let it out of his hands and kept showing me different maps, telling me how he would use the book with his students. One of the female teachers started reading the Harriet Tubman book and would not let it go. I was so thrilled seeing the smiles on their faces.

Duncan and I met with Joseph (the headmaster) and Henry (the assistant headmaster and class eight teacher) about the new scholarship fund I was starting. They had a few questions, and we set up a meeting to go over all of it with the class eight parents, guardians, and students the following Monday, July 18, at 9:30 a.m. I was really looking forward to this meeting.

I could not get it out of my mind how difficult all their lives were, and it was affecting me much more than it had two years earlier. It was so hard to see all of this again, when I knew how very different life was for so many people in the world.

I sat in on a number of classes in the afternoon, noticing how many of the inefficiencies in teaching were the result of a lack of resources, dirty and cramped classrooms, and the noise that came from other classes and from students running and screaming outside, since there was nothing to block the sound. Of course they also had no electricity. I saw some teachers who did a very good job, but some of the younger ones seemed lost. Because of all the distractions, it was hard for the teachers to get the full attention of all the students.

By and large, the students were amazing in terms of their willingness to listen, behave properly, take notes, and be respectful of the teacher. Virtually all of them seemed to take their education seriously. The older ones definitely had a sense that the only thing that was going to make their lives better was getting a great education. The reality was that without a high school education, their lives probably would not be any different than their parents'.

July 14, 2011

My entire day was spent at school, with a break for lunch. I watched many different classes and took some great videos. Also, today was the day to distribute some baseball T-shirts that had been donated by a family at the school where I taught. Mama Pamela took me over to the orphanage and gave each of the children a T-shirt. For the little ones, they were more like pajamas. Later in the day, I gave the rest of the T-shirts to the class eight students, and luckily I had just enough for all of them. I took a lot of great pictures of both events for the people back home. The children really appreciated the gifts, as they rarely if ever got something that was new and not a hand-me-down or from a charity.

Today was also the day that my dad would have been eighty-four years old. I thought a lot about him and the scholarship program I was starting in his and my mom's names. I knew they would have been proud, and I was thrilled to be able to memorialize them this way.

After the regular school day was over, I watched a debate that students from classes six, seven, and eight took part in. They acted as formally as members of parliament, and many of them had specific roles. They debated the merits of urban versus rural life. I was very impressed with how well organized they were and the many great points that were made on both sides. When I returned to my room, I found that some new volunteers had arrived. I met Hollie and her teenage daughter, Aziza, who were from California. It would be nice to have some other volunteers to talk to and share some time with. I also needed to charge my computer, phone, and camera. Mama Pamela and Duncan had solar power at night for a few hours and a power strip so that was when I could charge up.

July 15, 2011

It was another fascinating day, and I wanted to remember every minute of it. When we arrived at school about 7:20 a.m., the students were busy getting ready for their day. They were all in the school courtyard, and at 8:00 a.m. some students started marching in for the flag ceremony. They marched to the flagpole in the center of the courtyard and raised the Kenyan flag. The students then sang the national anthem.

Next began what they called the "pastoral program," where class eight students led all the other students in prayer and songs. This went on for about thirty-five minutes, and the students loved it. It was very inspirational. I then went back to Mama Pamela and Duncan's for some great breakfast and conversation.

I also finished a project I'd started the day before, getting the class seven and eight students to answer some questions about themselves on a piece of paper. I asked them things like their name, family information, what they wanted to be when they grew up, what they wanted people in the United States to know about people in Kenya, and so forth. My plan was to share their answers with my students back home, to help them better understand what life was like in Dago.

I watched some more lessons, and then we had lunch. After that, Edwin, Duncan's oldest son, took us on an awesome walk. I had been hearing a lot about the drought, and Edwin showed us the maize and other crops that were to be harvested soon. They were in very bad condition, and a poor crop would make a very bad food situation even worse. Kenya was having major problems with food shortages; I had seen stories on Kenyan TV about how the government was going out and buying maize (the country's main staple) from other countries. Edwin told us about a family of eleven in the area who had not had any food in two days. It was hard to take this news, but I began to realize that for Kenyans this was just part of everyday life and nothing out of the ordinary. We met a lady who was the oldest person in the village, and she had not eaten in two days. We did end up going to get some food and bringing it to all these people.

The field Edwin showed us was on a hill, and at the bottom of the hill was a river. I asked him about irrigation, since it seemed so sad that these crops were in such bad condition due to lack of water, when there was a river right at the bottom of the hill. Edwin said there was no way he could afford the cost of irrigation. He also mentioned that this river, which ten years earlier had been about five feet deep, was now only several inches deep. This was the first time I heard the term *global warming* spoken in Kenya, as Edwin explained that it was having a negative effect here.

He also took us on a tour of the new crops they had begun growing since I was there two years earlier. They were quite impressive. We looked at the new barn, which was right by the orphanage and housed the two cows my students had bought for Dago. We also met Bartlett and Linda. (Since the money for the cows had come from Bartlett High School students, I had asked that one of the cows be named Bartlett. Linda was the name of another volunteer from Chicago who had been a great help to Dago.) It was heartwarming to hear how these cows were benefiting the community and how they would be of even greater benefit when they had calves. This is a great example of how some American students can raise money that ends up having a phenomenal impact on the lives of children thousands of miles away.

We arrived back at school in time to see students cleaning up the room and the entire compound. Then they had the closing ceremony and took down the Kenyan flag. I saw the pride these people had in their country and hoped that this pride would bring a better life for all Kenyans.

July 16, 2011

I woke up early to take a really good tub shower and wash my hair. I felt so much cleaner when it was all done. After breakfast, we took a short walk of about three blocks to attend a church service that started at 9:30 a.m. and lasted until 1:00 p.m. Most of the people in Dago were Seventh-day Adventists, and the flow of the service was very similar to that of other religious services I had attended. Most of it was in their tribal language of Luo, but they did translate some parts of it into English for their guests from the United States. Each of us—Hollie, Aziza, and I—were asked to stand up and introduce ourselves to the members. At the end of the service, everyone went outside and stood in a circle, people went around the circle to greet each other individually, and then some final comments were made.

After that we ate lunch, and I went over my plans for the Monday meetings. Later we went over to the home of Duncan's father and stepmother. I learned some things about polygamy, which still existed in Kenya in some ways. Duncan's dad had more than one wife, and Duncan's mom had passed away. Duncan seemed embarrassed to tell me this, and I learned that people like Duncan and Mama Pamela were trying to create a new culture in which polygamy was not allowed.

July 17, 2011

Sunday was a bit of a different day in Dago. While the people told me it would be a day of relaxation for them, I never really saw them relax. The first thing I did was take some time to wash my clothes. I did two buckets' worth, with another bucket for rinsing, and then hung my clothes on the line to dry. It was nice to have all my clothes clean, at least by Kenyan standards.

I spent several hours with Edwin, as he and I always had great conversations. He was now thirty-one and planning to marry a Muslim lady he'd met in Nairobi. Edwin, of course, was a Christian, but this did not seem to bother his parents at all. I was surprised but happy to hear this. Edwin did say that it was a big issue for her father, whom he had not yet met. Edwin was working on getting the opportunity to meet him and ask for his blessing.

Edwin and I talked a lot about his future. Later that day he was going to an Internet café to see if he had been accepted into a medical program that would allow him to become a general doctor. He said that if he did not get into the program, he might have to give up on his idea for additional education. He was bright and talented and had so much to give his country, which needed so much. I hoped he got the chance to become everything he was capable of becoming.

I then learned why electronics were so expensive in Kenya—usually two or three times as expensive as they were in the United States, and quite often even more. It was all because of the high taxes the government put on these goods. It was pretty much impossible for most Kenyans to afford them. This was just another reason I was frustrated with the Kenyan government. I talk a lot about how nice the Kenyan people are, and in many ways I think their niceness really hurts them. They get frustrated with their government, but for the most part they just seem to accept it as a part of life. I am thinking they need to adopt the phrase from the movie *Network*: "I'm mad as hell and I am not going to take it anymore." I guess their lives are full of so many struggles it is hard to really take on this task.

Edwin had a number of ideas for new businesses that he might pursue if he didn't get into the medical program. We talked a lot about business and its challenges. Of course, his major problem would be getting enough capital to start a business—something that seemed to be in short supply in Kenya.

I then went over to the school, where classes six, seven, and eight were having lessons for a few hours in the afternoon, even though it was Sunday. After that I walked over to the orphanage, as the orphans would be returning from their weekend at "home." From the orphanage I could watch the Dago football (soccer) and netball teams practice for the upcoming Kick It in Kenya tournament, which would be held in August. This would be the third tournament, and I well remembered being there two years earlier for the first one.

Later at dinner, Duncan and I began preparing for the class eight students and parents meeting about the scholarship fund. I was really looking forward to it. Duncan and I also got into a conversation I had been hoping we would have. The conversation was about caning, or a teacher hitting a student with a cane. While I had not seen a lot of this in schools in Kenya, there had been several occasions when I saw a teacher hit a student either with a slap or a tree branch. It was always greatly disturbing to me and other volunteers when we saw this happen. I always tried to balance my thoughts on this subject with my not wanting to be the volunteer who comes to Africa to tell people how they should be living their lives. We all know that hitting students is a part of the history of every culture and society in the world. I slowly entered into this conversation, telling Mama Pamela and Duncan how uncomfortable it made me feel when I saw a student being hit, and my reasons for being against the practice. I was very nervous about bringing this up, as I did not want to offend them. Hollie chimed in with similar thoughts.

Duncan explained to me that while it was now against the law in Kenya to cane or hit a student, apparently the law was enforced only in Nairobi, the country's capital and largest city. Out in the villages and countryside, the old tradition of caning continued. During our conversation, both Duncan and Mama Pamela did some defending of the practice. Part of this defense included the statement that they had been caned when they were in school and had turned out very well. By the end of this conversation, they both said that as there was a need to make so many changes in Kenya, they knew that caning would eventually go away. I was relieved to hear them say this.

July 18, 2011

After breakfast this morning I began getting ready for my 9:30 a.m. meeting with the class eight students and parents about the scholarship fund. Duncan would interpret for me, as the parents' understanding of English could vary a great deal. Also, I wanted to come away with a picture and name for each of the class eight students so I could have this information when we got the applications at the end of the year.

Tomorrow I was going to start focusing more and more on my trip to Rwanda, which would be my destination after I left Kenya. I would be pursuing information on the Rwandan genocide, per my passion for studying and teaching about genocide. That is not part of what this book is about, but it may be the subject of another book.

After breakfast we headed over to the school for the meeting. I had butterflies in my stomach; this entire plan for the scholarship fund was so important to me. Even though I am a nut for having everything start on time, I knew enough about Kenya by now to know that almost everything and everyone runs late. I also knew that to get to the school, parents had to leave their work and walk a long distance. By 9:30 a.m., only one parent had arrived. By 10:00 a.m., twelve parents were there, so Duncan decided it was time to start. We went into the class eight room, and up front were several teacher's chairs the students had brought in for Hollie, Aziza, and me. Also sitting with us were the class eight teachers and the headmaster. As we were getting going, two more parents showed up, and then all the parents sat along the sides of the classroom, with the students in the middle. I then started the presentation about my parents, Bernard and Elsie Weiss, who'd grown up very poor in Chicago and wanted a college education but could not afford it. I went into what I had learned about the Kenyan system of education, and how I'd noticed that few children went to high school, especially children from Dago. As I was talking, I would stop every minute or two while Duncan translated what I was saying into Luo, so all the parents would understand.

I explained the rules of the program, our expectations, and the application process and timing. We wanted the students to know that if they got a scholarship, it meant we had committed to them for four years and had enough money in the bank for their full education. However, they needed to understand that we would review each student each year, and if they were not keeping their marks (grades) up, we reserved the right to take the scholarship away.

The parents had a number of questions after I was done talking, and many of them made some very nice comments, thanking me for doing this. As I listened to the parents say thank you, I had to wipe away a number of tears. It was a very emotional moment for me, almost overwhelming, and made me think a lot about my late mom and dad.

Next it was time to take a picture of each of the class eight students, and Hollie and Aziza helped me get them to write down their names in the order in which I was taking the pictures, so when I got back home I could match up the right pictures with the right names. This went pretty quickly, and then I shook hands with each parent and each of the thirty students. The entire event lasted about ninety minutes.

As I walked away, my emotions were boiling over. The meeting I'd just gone through made all my planning, hopes, and dreams about this scholarship program very real and official. I was so excited to begin the process of trying to help some of these excellent students. I would be raising money so that at the end of the year we could award scholarships to as many of these students as possible.

I watched a few more classes before going back home for some lunch. I spent the afternoon at the orphanage, watching the meeting that Mama Pamela was having with her workers and mentors, who reached out to all the families in the area to make sure their needs were being met and help them out if they were not. This was very similar to a meeting I had attended two years earlier; however, a big difference was that back then, the workers and mentors received a monthly stipend from a US government grant. Now they no longer had this grant, so each of these women was doing the work without pay, motivated only by the passion she had for trying to help her community. Both Hollie and I talked to the women about how impressed we were with the work they are doing, and even more so now, since they were doing it for free. After an emotional morning, it was an inspiring afternoon.

July 19, 2011

It was my second-to-last full day in Dago, as Thursday morning I would leave to go back to Nairobi so I could catch my flight to Kigali, Rwanda. I wanted to spend some more time with the students at the school before I left. However, I found out that classes three through eight would be taking exams, so I was not sure how much time I would actually get with the students. I'd been thinking a lot about how hard each of these students worked. The older primary children seemed to have a reasonable understanding of how crucial education was for them. They understood that without a high school education, their lives would probably not be any different than their parents'—lives of absolute poverty. When I asked students to write their biographies, one of my questions was what they wanted to do for a living. Every student wrote down some kind of white-collar profession, such as a doctor, lawyer, teacher, engineer, nurse, or pilot. The very sad reality was that the vast majority of them would probably never even come close to achieving these dreams. I am not saying this to be negative, but just to be realistic. In doing what I was going to try to do, I was hoping I could create a few more well-educated people who could help the country of Kenya and also "pay it forward" to other young Kenyans. The country's problems were so deep, pervasive, and overwhelming, you could only hope for small, incremental changes, piece by piece.

There seemed to me to be a new spirit of optimism in Kenya with the previous year's passage of a new constitution. People seemed to believe that this document could help bring about more democracy, equality, and fairness, both political and economic, for all Kenyans. They also hoped that this new constitution could greatly decrease the corruption that seemed to be everywhere in Kenyan society.

By and large, the people were nice and worked incredibly hard. Each of them just wanted a chance at a better life. The sad reality is that, quite often, hard work alone will not result in a better life. People like Mama Pamela and Duncan were so inspirational. If they wanted to, they could have led lives of (relative Kenyan) luxury. However, they chose to give most of their time and resources back to their community, to give the children a real chance at better lives. They were all so positive and optimistic. As I told my own students, these people, for me, were examples of real heroes in our world. Oh well ... it was time for me to resume cleaning up and packing.

After the cleaning and packing, I took a really nice tub shower. Then Edwin returned, saying he had not gotten into the medical program he had hoped for. He was very disappointed; however, as

I'd seen so often with Kenyans, he seemed to be taking it pretty well. I was a bit surprised, because I knew how much he wanted this. He told me that he now needed to focus on just making a living, and that he was probably going to lease some land with a friend of his in order to grow some crops to sell next year. He said he hoped to take those profits to open up a "stationary shop" to sell office supplies in Kilgoris. He seemed excited and optimistic about his future, despite the bad news.

I spent the afternoon at school, talking to a lot of the students and teachers. I was telling them that tomorrow would be my last day in Dago. They were asking me questions like "When are you coming back?" and "Why don't you bring some of your students back here with you?" They went on and on with questions. They also asked me many questions about the United States. As I'd expected, they looked at the United States as a monolithic culture, and it was hard to get them to understand how diverse the United States is in terms of people, types of land, income levels, weather, and so on. I would have the same issues with the adults also.

I had a very interesting conversation with one of the teachers. We were standing by a mud hut the school used as a kitchen. It was right next to the small brick building the teachers used as their office. I need to explain that their "kitchen" was something very different than what we Americans would call a kitchen. It was really just a mud hut with a place to make a fire so they could cook food and heat water. The teacher asked me about the mud huts in the United States. I was not quite sure how to respond, but then I told her that we did not have any mud huts in the United States. She was in absolute shock when I told her this. I do not think she could imagine a country that did not have mud huts. And this was a teacher, not one of the students.

I then had another talk with Edwin, who helped me better understand the difference between public and private primary schools in Kenya. He told me that private school students tended to score better on the KCPE, but public school students tended to do better in high school. The reason, he said, was because the private school students tended to have all their time structured by the school and thus did not know how to use their free time when they got to high school. However, public school students were used to having free time and thus had to learn early how to make good use of it; as a result, they did better in high school. In my future work in Kenya, I would learn that there were a variety of opinions on this matter, and not everyone would agree with Edwin.

July 20, 2011

This was my last full day in Dago. There was another incredibly beautiful sunrise over the hills in the east. The rolling hills here were just gorgeous. All the sounds that made this part of the world so unique could be heard, from the roosters to the many kinds of birds, to the cows and goats and of course the barking dogs. Many of the children had already made it to school, and people were already working hard in the fields. When I listened carefully, I could hear the sound of their machetes. It was all so memorable, and now that I had heard it all so many times, even when I got back home it would play in my head like a recording that lasts forever.

I'd had an incredible time during this trip to Dago and had accomplished everything and more I had come here to do. I had learned so much about how I could improve myself as a human being and a teacher. Yes, there were many things these folks need to learn from us, but we in the West needed to understand there was much we needed to learn from them too. The Kenyans take life at an easier pace, enjoying each and every moment. They really take the time to appreciate and love family and friends. They eat only fresh food, and with the big trend toward organic farming here, they eat very healthily. There is no such thing as junk food here. And everyone, from the children to the adults, works very hard each and every day. I never really heard them complain about their lives, despite all the obstacles that confront them each day. They never seem to lose their optimism about the future, and they never give up. They want so badly for life to be better for their children.

I knew the future here would not be dramatically better in a week, in a month, or in a year. However I was convinced that it would get better and that the people of Kenya were on the right track. As more and more people became aware and educated, they would force their government to be more honest and efficient. They would demand better from their government.

I was going to do whatever I could to help and, I hope, inspire others to help too. The Kenyans were not looking for people to give them things; they just wanted a real chance to improve their lives. They wanted some of the obstacles to be removed so they could reap the benefits they deserved from all their hard work. I hoped I would be around long enough to see real and substantive changes in Kenya.

I would be spending my morning at school, and then after lunch I would say my good-byes. In the afternoon, I would take time to finish packing, do laundry, shave, and so forth. I would walk around the compound a few more times, just to take it all in. Then, at about 7:30 tomorrow morning, Edwin and I would leave for Nairobi. From past experience, I knew this journey could take anywhere from six to eight hours. I would be at Wendy's home Thursday night, and if I had time, I would get on the Internet at her house. I would fly out of Jomo Kenyatta Airport around 8:30 a.m. Friday to go to Kigali, Rwanda. I was a bit nervous, because there had been many stories in the news about blackouts at the Nairobi airport that had canceled many flights. Lately it looked like things were better, but I knew the power in Nairobi was always a bit shaky, so I was hoping this would not affect my ability to get to Rwanda on time.

Thus my time in Kenya for 2011 came to an end—and the Bernard and Elsie Weiss Dago Scholarship Fund officially began!

> Faith is taking the first step even when you
> don't see the whole staircase.
> —Martin Luther King Jr.

Kenya 2013 Trip

I would like to create projects that will bring income to
my community. The projects will include beekeeping,
dairy and fish farming, and poultry keeping.
I will offer scholarships to the orphans and to
the children whose parents are disabled.
—Moses, scholarship recipient

June 14, 2013

After traveling through Amsterdam, I arrived in Nairobi to begin
my third journey to Kenya. I was spending the night at Wendy and
Martin's home (Wendy was now married to Martin), and everything
went perfectly. For the first time in my three trips to Kenya, all my
luggage actually arrived at the same time I did. It was 10:30 p.m.,
and Wendy made a great dinner. We had to be out at 7:30 a.m.,
so I needed to get to sleep. We would be taking a bus for a long
journey to the northwest part of Kenya, to a town called Kitale.
Joshua Machinga, from an organization called Common Ground,
would be meeting us to take me to his home. It appeared as though
it would be about an eight-hour ride. I was very excited to be able
to meet Joshua, with whom I had been Facebook friends for a couple
of years. I had been told that he ran one of the best primary schools
in all of Kenya, and I looked forward to learning a lot from him. I
was anxious to see what how his school was similar to and different

from Emmanuel's private school that I'd visited two years earlier. I would be in Kitale for a few days and then would return to Dago, which from my understanding was about a three-hour drive from Joshua's home.

June 15, 2013

I was up at 6:30 a.m., and at 7:30 a.m. Wendy's driver took us to downtown Nairobi to catch our bus. I was happy to find out that this was a real bus and not just another matatu. It was a pretty nice bus with comfortable seats, and I was happy about that for this eight-hour drive. We stopped a couple of times for some breaks. They took great care of me and all my luggage.

Joshua met me when we arrived in Kitale, along with a guy who worked for him and a couple of other volunteers who were working on projects. One was from Calgary and the other was from New York. We drove about ten miles to the village of Kiminini, where Joshua's Pathfinder Academy was located. I settled into a very nice room that had full power, real bathrooms, and a nice shower like the one at Wendy and Martin's house. From my experience in Kenya, this was like a four-star hotel.

Joshua gave me a tour of the grounds. He had about five hundred students in classes one through eight. About half the students lived on the school grounds. Also on the compound there was a real nice guesthouse (I was staying in one of the rooms), dorms, and classrooms. Joshua's background was in agriculture, so they grew most of their own food. He also had a ceramics factory that made water filters.

Then we all had dinner, and I was able to talk to Joshua quite a bit. Even though his background was in agriculture, he'd started his own school about sixteen years earlier because he was so frustrated with the schools in Kenya. He told me that he would be a horrible teacher but he did know how to run a school. His students did incredibly well on the KCPE. His average score was far higher than those of any of the Dago students of the last two years. His school, like Emmanuel's, got all its money from tuition and donations, much like a private school in the United States.

It was very clear that he pushed his teachers and students to work hard each and every day. When I asked him where he got his teachers, he said he got to view all the test scores of Kenya's class eight students and could see whom the teachers were. He then "poached" (his word, not mine) the teachers whose students had the best scores. He said he paid his teachers more than they were making before, and they had the second-best pay in all of Kenya.

I was really looking forward to getting to know more about Joshua and his school during the next few days. But first I needed to get some sleep.

June 16, 2013

This morning I had the "grand tour" from Joshua of everything going on at the compound, and it was marvelous, all the things he was involved with. This was so much more than just a primary school with five hundred students, about half of them boarders. Joshua had made major investments in water systems, solar power, and farming to help the place become almost self-reliant. His farm was totally organic, and he controlled every little detail to make everything very efficient. He told me he'd had to learn a lot about solar power and water systems.

As he showed me all of this, I could not help but think like an economist and consider the important concept of specialization. In my world, I did not have to have any idea how power got to my house. When I wanted food, I went to the grocery store or a restaurant. When I wanted water, I just turned the tap, and of course I paid the bills for all these items. Here, because the government was so poor, inept, corrupt, and inefficient, everyone had to reinvent the wheel. Now, Joshua had reinvented the wheel far better than anyone else I had met during my time in Kenya. I couldn't help but think, though, how sad it was that he had to do this.

In the United States, schools can focus almost totally on delivering education to their students. Joshua and others who do what he does have to do so much more than just focus on education. They have to make sure all the resources necessary to run the school are available. This is a great example to give my students to illustrate the importance of specialization in an advanced society. Schools in my world are blessed to have most of the resources they need readily available to them without any worry.

I told Joshua he was a master at marketing. He got so much money from so many different places and organizations, and he was great about getting on planes to visit them and keeping in touch with them via Facebook and e-mail. It was clear that he had a lot of people who felt very good about what he was doing, because they kept giving him money. Obviously he was producing great results and getting rewarded for his success. While it was clear that he had a lot to teach others about agriculture, water supply, and solar power systems, he also had a lot he could teach others about marketing and raising money.

Joshua then drove me a few miles to some land where he planned to build a high school for girls. Some of this land he was now using for farming. He took me through a couple of acres, explaining about the different crops and how he worked to maximize the return on everything he planted. This led to more discussion of the advantages of organic farming. Needless to say, he was very much in favor of organic, for both the farmer and the consumer.

We then began discussing his new high school for girls, which would open in January 2014. A big part of what was driving him to open the school was all the costs he had incurred helping children get a high school education. I shared with him my frustration about having to pay fees for a high school education, and how you got a bill in January that was supposed to be for the entire year, but you knew the school would add on various charges during the year. He also would have preferred paying one bill upfront and, you know, that's it for the year. He explained to me that part of the problem was the government, which made promises about giving money to the schools but then did not follow through on those promises. I told him that on my trip I would bring up this point when I visited the five high schools Dago children were attending. I was going to tell them how not having a fixed cost upfront made it more difficult for people like me to help, and I'd explain that having one fee that did not change was what we were used to in the United States. Joshua said he thought they would be polite and listen, but then tell me that they couldn't do anything. Another issue I would bring up was the fact that when costs like these changed, it was hard to know if the school was taking advantage of the fact that someone from the United States was sponsoring the child in question. It was a tough issue.

We moved on to discuss his girls' high school, which would be called Lenana—the same name as a local boys' high school that had a very good reputation. Apparently there was no issue here with just using another school's name. He said the fact that people felt so positive about that school would help convince people to send their daughter to his school. As I kept telling him, he was great at marketing.

He wanted to start his first year with twenty-five standard one (freshmen) students. He wanted to start small, to create great successes right up front. He would hire three teachers and a principal to work the first year. He would have a very low student-to-staff ratio to make sure each of the twenty-five students got a great education. Then as word spread about how well these students were doing, more and more parents would send their girls there. He wanted to include some students from his Pathfinder Primary School; however, his top priority would be students who scored well on the KCPE and had great character.

We then talked about his philosophy of what a school should be. He was a big believer that schools didn't just have to do a great job teaching students in each of the subject areas, but they also had to do a great job preparing them for the real world. He went on to talk about how students needed "practical skills" in order to make a living. He said he would only accept students who were willing to "get their hands dirty," meaning that they would learn all the things they needed to know about how to be successful and efficient farmers. Thus he wanted his school to combine the best of both an academic and a vocational education. And from what I had seen so far, I thought he would be very successful.

Joshua pushed his teachers and students a great deal. Education here was basically a seven-days-a-week operation, and each of the Monday-through-Friday school days was very long. And as with other schools in Kenya, this one ran pretty much all year round. Clearly education was taken very seriously here, and I knew that those of us in education in the United States could learn a lot from Joshua and his staff. He mentioned that a former student of his was going to begin his freshman year at Stanford University in the fall.

I then asked a number of questions about high schools throughout Kenya. I asked if he thought the number of Kenyan children attending high school had improved in recent years. He was not sure about that, but he said his gut told him that one-fourth of Kenyan children of high school age were actually attending.

Joshua then told me that many people approached him to ask how he was so successful, because they wanted to replicate what he did. We then talked about how the fact that his was a private school was a key part of its success. He was not dependent on money from the government; he fundraised for his money. I told him that private schools in the United States had an advantage because they could pick and keep the students they wanted, where public schools did not have that option. It seemed like schools like his and Emmanuel's had this same kind of advantage, but it may not have been as big a deal in Kenya.

On a different topic, we saw many people on their way to and from church, so this led to a discussion of the various religions in the area and how everyone got along. He and his family were Seventh-day Adventists (just like most of the people in Dago) and went to church on Saturday. He had services right at the school for all the children and adults who lived on campus. The service was run by a youth minister on his staff. Since today was Sunday, the people going to and from church were from other Christian religions, including

Catholics and various Protestant groups. He said that there was also a Muslim community in the area and that some of his students were Muslim. I told him about my work with the Children of Abraham Coalition, bringing Jewish, Christian, and Muslim students together to promote learning about people of different religions and to create a world of tolerance and understanding between these groups. He then told me that his church had been doing something similar, bringing together Muslim and Christians for the same purpose.

He then gave me a tour of his property. We discussed the violence that had occurred in some parts of Kenya, including this area, in 2007, as a result of anger about the presidential election results. Much of the anger was between the Kikuyu, which was the largest of all the tribes in Kenya, and the Luo (the people in Dago were Luo), which was the second- or third-largest tribe, depending on which data you were looking at. The Kikuyu had been the most politically powerful tribe since Kenya became a country. The candidate who came in second was a Luo. There were accusations of cheating, which started the trouble. Joshua came from a very small tribe.

As Joshua was walking me around his property, he started talking about two hut-like buildings that he had once used for guests like me. I was staying in a building that could house up to sixteen guests, as opposed to those, which were for two guests. One of the huts burned down as a result of the 2007 violence. When I asked him why, he said that most of the violence was anti-Kikuyu, and that some people in the area did not like the fact that Joshua never asked school families what tribe they were from. As a result, he had Kikuyu students, and he was approached by people asking him not to allow Kikuyu children into his school. When he refused to do that, he was attacked.

The whole matter of the 2007 violence was something I'd been learning more and more about over the past few years, as I continued my education on Kenya. Today I had learned a great deal more. Tensions between tribes were a big issue in Kenya, although it seemed like things were getting better. It did not seem to be anything like the tensions between the Hutu and Tutsis that led to the 1994 genocide in Rwanda. Also, earlier that year, Kenya had its first presidential election since 2007, and even though a Kikuyu won, there was only minimal violence in the country as a result of the election.

Tomorrow would be the first regular school day since I arrived, and I was looking forward to seeing and learning a great deal more. On Wednesday there was a district singing event going on—a district seemed to be like a county in the United States—and I was really looking forward to seeing it.

June 17, 2013

I spent the morning at the Pathfinder Academy Primary School, meeting many of the teachers and students. I watched the opening ceremony, including the flag ceremony and opening comments by a number of the teachers. This ceremony was just like similar events I had seen in Dago and at Emmanuel's school. They asked me to address the students by introducing myself and telling them about myself.

I spent the rest of the morning meeting with various classes. I asked the older children what they wanted to know about the United States, and this led to a number of excellent questions. Their main questions were about things like how job opportunities in the United States compared to those in Kenya, what differences there were in the weather, whether caning or hitting students was allowed in the United States, the types of food Americans ate, American tourist attractions, and the like.

I was back at Pathfinder Academy that afternoon. I spent about two hours in a class seven social studies lesson, answering more questions about the United States. The group had one question after another, and when our time together had ended, I think they could have gone on and on. Another common question, one I got all the time in Kenya, was about poverty in the United States. The children really viewed the United States as a place with no poverty. When I explained that we did have poor people, they were always very surprised. I then always had to explain that poverty in the United States was very different from poverty in Kenya. Poverty in the United States was almost like being middle class in Kenya.

After this, most of the students got together in a large room, and various groups that would be singing in the tournament in a couple of days practiced their performances. After watching them, I would call the tournament more of a singing and poetry contest.

I was back in my room a bit after 5:00 p.m., and the day had clearly exhausted me, as I fell right asleep and stayed asleep until about 7:00 p.m. At that point I went to dinner and enjoyed conversation in a combination of English and Kiswahili. Joshua wanted to take me to a village the next day, so I was sure it would be another fascinating day.

I remembered something I'd thought about quite often during my first two visits here. One day in Kenya was like week for me, because so much of what was happening was so new and different. Now it was Monday evening—I had only been here since Saturday night—but I felt like I had been here for at least a week. I decided that no matter how many times I came here, each minute would be filled with so much that nothing would ever feel routine. Each moment I thought deeply about the differences between life back home and life here in Kenya, and they were enormous. However, at the same time I was always reminded that people are people and children are children, wherever you go in this world. The things we have in common as human beings are always far greater than our differences. And we all need to celebrate our differences, because they are what make each of us unique and special. We all have so much to learn from one another. More and more I advise young people to visit many countries around the globe and get to know people. They should spend quality, substantive time with people of different religions, cultures, nationalities, and tribes. Surely the way to a peaceful world is for us to get to know each other, regardless of our backgrounds.

Tuesday, June 18, 2013

This morning we stopped over at the ceramics factory in the compound that Joshua ran. I'd seen it on Saturday, but Joshua wanted me to see it when the guys were actually working and making the ceramic water filters. The guys showed me how they made the filters a couple of times, and then, to my surprise, they told me that I was going to make one. Well, anyone who knows me knows I am no good with anything that has to do with mechanics or making things, so I was really nervous. I did make two of them, and there were several steps in the process. The guys were very nice and helped a lot when I was stuck, which was quite often. Joshua took some good pictures of me fumbling my way through trying to make the water filters.

We came back to the compound for a while, and then Joshua walked me into the center of the village of Kiminini. I talked to a number of the merchants in this area, where all kinds of food, clothing, and other things were being sold. I met a young man who was wearing a Chicago Bulls cap with the number twenty-three on it. I mentioned Michael Jordan, and his eyes lit up. When I told him I was from Chicago, he got even more excited. He was selling what I understood to be rolls of brown sugar. Of course he wanted me to buy some from him, but with his best sales hat on, he said instead that I could have a sample and that I would love it so much I would want to buy a lot. Well, looking at the rolls of sugar, which had a variety of insects crawling all over them, I found it hard to say much, but I did manage to say, "Thanks but no thanks." As all Kenyans seem to do, he took my rejection well, shook my hand, and told me that he hoped I enjoyed my stay there and that I should come back.

Then Joshua had someone from Pathfinder Academy drive the school van to the center of the village to pick us up. We brought along two young ladies—one I think worked for Joshua, and the other was an intern. We drove for about fifteen minutes way off the main road, down some really bumpy dirt roads to the home of a woman. This was going to be a meeting of a group of widows

Joshua helped out. They met twice a month and pooled their money to purchase items that could help all of them, kind of like a co-op. There were twenty-five women in the group, and fourteen showed up for the meeting. I got a kick out of the fact that they'd placed a little jar at the front door of the hut, and any woman who was late had to pay a fine. I especially enjoyed this because I knew from my time there that Kenyans were always late.

Joshua helped these women by giving them matching grants. When there was something they wanted to buy and they had enough money to pay half, then Joshua would put up the other half, but it was a loan that had to be repaid. The meeting began with each woman putting up some money for various funds they had. Most of the speaking was in Kiswahili, but every now and then Joshua would do some interpreting in English so I would understand what was going on. They had discussions about what they would do with the money and about farming techniques. Joshua had many talents, but teaching about agriculture was where he really excelled, since this was the subject of his degree and much of his life experience. We went outside the host's home to look at her banana trees; they were looking pretty bad, and Joshua scolded her. The meeting reminded me a bit of two women's groups I'd met with when I was in Rwanda two years earlier, except this one dealt strictly with agriculture as a means of making a living.

I had become fascinated learning about farming in Kenya, another of so many subjects here I knew so little about. Joshua said that he could teach a family to grow using his methods, and if they used them they could feed an entire family of eight with just one-eighth of an acre, as opposed to the "other" way of farming, which required two to three acres. In a country where so much of the problem was that almost all families had to grow their own food but many had very little land on which to do so, Joshua's plan was crucial to creating a society where everyone had enough to eat.

That afternoon I had a very special time, as Joshua had me sit down with an extraordinary group of students. In the Pathfinder Academy, class eight students were divided into three classes. One was

121

called preform one. The first year of high school was called form one, so what these preform students were doing this year was all the work regular class eight students did, including getting ready for the KCPE, as well as some form one work to give them a head start on secondary school. These students were all girls because Joshua wanted them all to attend the all-girls' high school (Lenana Girls High School) that he was starting in January. In the area that was kind of like a living room in the front of the building where my room was, we all sat and talked. Joshua wanted me to ask the girls questions to start a discussion, so I asked things like "What are your hopes for the Kenya of the future?" and "What would you say to President Kenyatta if you had a chance to talk to him?" I also asked that same question about President Obama. One of the girls was from the same village that President Obama's dad was from. I asked each of the girls what she wanted to be when she grew up. All of this led to many interesting discussions about the world and questions about the United States. We went into the topic of automation because they were fascinated to hear how, in the rest of the world, machines had taken over so much of the work that in Kenya was done by people. They were a fascinating and fun group of youngsters to talk to, and I have to admit that by the end of it I felt very good about the future of Kenya.

Wednesday, June 19, 2013

I spent this entire day at the County Music and Poetry Festival, and it was sensational. There were roughly fifty primary schools attending. I took many pictures and videos of the eight performances by the children from Joshua's Pathfinder Academy. They had an amazing day, coming in first in five of the categories and second in two of them. First and second places allowed a group to go to the next round, the regionals at the end of the month, so all the students were very excited, as their hard work had really paid off. It was fun seeing all the different students with their various uniforms and costumes. There was a lot of great talent on display.

After the performances, Moses, the assistant principal of the school, walked me into the town of Kitale. This was by far the most modern city I had been to in Kenya. It was a city of about one hundred thousand people. The entire city had electricity, and the downtown area had the nicest-looking shops I had seen in Kenya. There were banks everywhere I looked; most of them were British. We ate dinner at the Iroko Boulevard Restaurant, which was by far the best restaurant I had ever eaten at in Kenya, other than the restaurant where I ate two years earlier on safari. That was not what I would really call a real Kenyan restaurant, though. Some things in Kenya are very expensive to Americans, and some are very inexpensive. Food is one thing that is a great bargain. I had a very nice chicken dinner with a small salad, soup, and *chapati* (unleavened bread). And as I was finishing, I found out I could get seconds for free, so I did. All of this cost about two hundred fifty Kenyan shillings, or about three US dollars.

I had a very interesting conversation with Moses, who was a retired secondary teacher. He'd come to work as an administrator at Pathfinder Academy after he retired. He had four children, and the oldest two were the same age as my children. His parents were alive and in their nineties, but his mom was very sick, having had a stroke. He was a very interesting and classy man to get to know and learn from.

I then ended my short time with Joshua at Common Ground and Pathfinder Academy. He was doing so many stunning things with his students and the community. He had solar power that worked most of the time for everyone. There was some Internet access too, and some real plumbing. He was getting great results from his students. Since his was a private school, like Emmanuel's, it had some of the same advantages private schools have in the United States. I learned that the reason this area of Kenya was so economically advanced was that it was the best area for farming in Kenya.

Joshua went after the best teachers in Kenya, and he was willing to pay those teachers more than what they were currently making, and he got great results. His school was in many ways similar to Emmanuel's, but the two men had very different backgrounds, and that difference was reflected in the way the schools were run. Emmanuel's background was in education and libraries, while Joshua's was in farming. So getting to know each of these schools allowed me to learn a lot more about education in this unfamiliar world called Kenya.

It was time for me to get some sleep; in the morning I would head back to Dago. I had been told it would be about a three-hour journey, but then I learned it was double that. Well, this was the way of life in Kenya.

Thursday, June 20, 2013

My journey to Dago was long and tough. It took more than nine hours. Kenyan time is always longer! From the village where I was staying, Kiminini, I boarded a pretty nice bus called Prince Coach. We drove about three and a half hours to Kisumu. I had my two carry-on bags and two large suitcases. In Kisumu we switched to a matatu, squeezing in along with many other people. My two large suitcases were tied to the top of the van along with other luggage, bags of grain, and so on. When everyone was squeezed in, other passengers just grabbed on to the sides of the matatu. Most of the time I just tried to get as comfortable as possible, put my head down, and prayed to God that I'd make it to my destination safely. We drove about three hours to Kisii, a city that I was very familiar with from my other visits. I then had to switch to another matatu, get all reloaded, and ride to the village of Ranen, which took another three hours. Part of why the matatus took so long was because they stopped for anyone who wanted to get on or off. And then there was the very poor condition of the Kenyan roads. "Awful" did not begin to describe them. Many times there was no road at all, just dirt and rocks. At times there were actually two lanes, and at other times just one. Sometimes there was not even one lane. And of course there were many very large potholes. Add to all this the fact that at any moment you could have large groups of animals crossing the road, and you never knew how long a journey might take.

George and Duncan met me at Ranen for the last mile or so up the dirt road to Dago. We used the guys on motorbikes to get me and my luggage there. I was shown to my room, where I unpacked and set things up so I could create my "routines," and then I went to Mama Pamela and Duncan's home. We sat down for some chai, great conversation, and dinner. In addition to George being with us, Edwin, who was now married, was there with his wife, Habiba, and son, Harun. Also, Felix, whom I'd last seen four years earlier, was home after graduating high school. He was waiting to hear from the government about a university. We had a great evening, and by 9:30 I was exhausted and went to bed.

Friday June 21, 2013

I was up by 6:00 a.m. to get going for the day. I gathered water and had my tub shower; that was the cleanest I would be in Dago. I walked over to the primary and nursery schools to visit the children and see how the area had changed since my last visit a couple of years ago. I then ate some breakfast, and we waited for George to come with our rental car. I'd given him money to rent a car from a place in Kisii and put some gas in it. Things were delayed as he was on the way to pick up Duncan and me in Dago; he had some trouble with the car and had to return it and get another one. I was anxious to begin my main mission on this trip: to visit each of our scholarship recipients at the school he or she attended.

Around 11:30 a.m., with George driving and Duncan in the front seat with him, we took off for the one-hour drive to see Roy at Agoro Sare High School. We had a fabulous time with Roy, who was in his second year there. We spent some real quality time with him, and he was about two inches taller than when we'd visited him two years earlier. We then met a man named George, the senior master of the school. We had an excellent meeting, and I came away with his name and e-mail address, along with the name and e-mail address of the dean of students, even though he was not available

125

for a meeting. One of my main goals for this trip was to come away with the names and e-mail addresses of the key people at each of the schools we visited, so I had a way to keep in touch with them from back home.

Overall, Roy was doing very well, although his grades were down a bit in this second year, what they called form two. One of the things Mama Pamela and Duncan help me out with was getting the report card for our students after each of their three terms every year. It had been explained to me that teachers got much tougher in form two and even tougher in form three. I talked to Roy about working even harder.

Duncan had a way of getting to a key point he wanted to make. At school, Roy and our other students lived in much better surroundings than they did in Dago. With our support, they got three good meals each day, a lot more books and supplies than they ever had in primary school, nice uniforms, and dorm rooms that were much better than the mud huts they lived in back home. Duncan began a speech with Roy that I would see repeated with the other students. He said, "Do you see the way people live in Dago? Do you want to go back to living that way? There is an even better way of life beyond high school if you are willing to work hard." This seemed to make a great impression on the students.

We made the drive back to Dago in a driving rainstorm. The Kenyan roads are bad enough on a nice day but become much worse in the rain. George had a really nice car for us to travel in, and he was an excellent driver, making his way around the potholes and other obstacles. For a long time I'd been nervous about how my visits to the five high schools and seven students would go. I felt great that we were off to a fantastic start.

Saturday, June 22, 2013

It was my birthday and I was in Dago, Kenya. So this would be a very different kind of birthday. I had learned that birthdays were not really a big deal in Kenya, probably because of the tremendous amount of poverty and how tough life was. Taking time to celebrate a birthday was not a high priority for most people. Edwin told me that if he had known it was my birthday, he would have sliced up a cow for me. He had a big smile on his face as he told me that.

This morning I did my wash for the first time since arriving in Kenya. As I have explained before, it was a long process involving buckets, pumping water, hand washing and rinsing, and then hanging the clothes up on the line to dry. It brought back memories of when I was little and we did not have a dryer and so hung our clothes to dry.

I then went to the Seventh-day Adventist church service. I'd sat through one a couple of years before when I was here, so I thought I would do it again. The service was about three hours long, and it was all in Luo, so I did not understand a word. The minister, whom I had met a few days earlier, asked me to get up and introduce myself to the people of the church. George brought a version of the King James Bible for me to use, and he would point to the proper places in the Bible so I could read the English version of what they were saying in Luo. He also explained other things that were happening. At the end of service, I saw a boy who was wearing one of the T-shirts I'd given out two years earlier from the Carol Stream baseball team, so I had to take a picture of him.

After church, several people started talking to me about how we should take a drive to Tanzania for my birthday. I told George and Edwin that I did not have a visa to enter Tanzania, so I did not think this was a good idea. However, against my better judgment, they convinced me to go. They told me it was about an hour's drive, and we could just take a short walk from the border into Tanzania and all would be okay. I made a few jokes about spending the night in a Tanzanian jail. As we left, they told me that I would probably be approached several times to pay a bribe but I should never, ever pay one.

When we got to the border, there was the Kenyan side, about thirty yards of a kind of middle ground, and then the Tanzanian side. On the Kenyan side, the guard told us we would have to pay

150 Kenyan shillings (about a $1.50) to go across. Edwin and George talked to him a bit in Swahili, and all of a sudden he just told us to go across. Edwin said the guard had been hoping we would pay the bribe, and when he realized we had no intention of paying, he just let us go.

Then as we crossed into Tanzania, of course there was a man in a uniform over by a building with a sign reading Immigration. He easily spotted the only muzungu and called us over. I became quite nervous and started thinking, *This is why I always make a point of keeping my passport on me.* Seeing that I was from the United States, he said, "You know you cannot just walk into another country without a visa." I was trying to say as little as possible and just listen very respectfully. He looked through my passport and, seeing my Kenyan visa, asked me what I was doing in Kenya. I told him my story and he said, "It is all right for Kenyans to come over, because they are our neighbors. Does the United States border Kenya?" Clearly he was trying to make a point. I responded, "No sir."

At that point I was not sure what would happen. He started talking to George and Edwin in Swahili. For about a minute it seemed very serious, and I was getting more and more worried. Would I be spending some time in a Tanzanian jail after all? All of a sudden the three of them were laughing. He looked at me very seriously and said I could go in, but only for one hour, and then I must cross back into Kenya. I said *asante* ("thanks") and started walking. We walked about a block and went into a restaurant, where we each had some soda. Mama Pamela and Edwin's wife and son, Habiba and Harun, were also with us. I kept looking at my watch, because I did not want to disobey my orders and we needed to be back in Kenya in less than an hour. As we were leaving the country, I made a point to catch the attention of the man from immigration to let him know I was leaving. We waved to each other. This became another interesting moment for me in Kenya. Looking back, it was probably not very smart to do what I did, but it all worked out just fine and made for a very memorable evening.

At the time, I told myself I was not going to tell Chris about it. I did not want her to worry about me, and I wanted her to know that I was always being careful and making good decisions. She would not take this as one of my best decisions. However, I am not very good about keeping secrets, and when I was back home, I did tell her.

We then made the drive back to Dago and got ready for dinner. Sunday would be a day of some relaxation and cleaning before we got back to the school visits on Monday. Also, tomorrow I wanted to give Mama Pamela some clothes I'd brought for the children.

Sunday, June 23, 2013

This was a day to relax, although for Kenyans there was really no such day. Most Kenyans were either full-time or part-time farmers, and crops and animals don't care what day it is. They still need to be taken care of. However, for me, it was a pretty relaxing day. After breakfast, Duncan and I spent most of the morning solving all of the world's problems. We both really enjoyed this kind of conversation. Also, there are many things to talk about when you're comparing life in Kenya and the United States. As we were talking, a man named Samuel came by, and he was a very interesting man to talk to and get to know. He worked for the government, assisting farmers. In discussing his personal life, he said he had eight children, the oldest of whom was thirty, and another child he took care of who was in class seven. He'd lost his wife several years earlier, so he had been the sole parent for all those children since then.

He took out some paperwork on the girl he was taking care of. It was from her primary school, and it showed that she was an excellent student, fourth in her class of thirty-eight. I knew from past experience that the schools were really big on all students knowing where they ranked compared to other students. He was worried about how he was going to pay for her high school. He did not live in Dago. He made the point several times that since he was a civil servant, he did not make much money.

He was a very interesting man, and I loved hearing him talk

about life in Kenya. I gave him my business card, and he promised to send me an e-mail. I took a picture of him and Duncan by his motorcycle just before he left. Of course the sad reality was there was nothing I could do to help him. He never did send me an e-mail.

Also, I went over a few things with Mama Pamela. She turned over receipts from the school payments and other costs incurred by the students in the scholarship program. This kind of accounting is always a complicated process, as I try very hard to have a receipt for every penny we spend, but in reality, if I can just come close to that goal, I am happy. Three of the five schools I owed money to, and I planned to review this with the school officials when we saw them over the upcoming week, and let them know we would get that money paid as soon as I got back home. The other two schools had said we were paid for the year, but I knew how things worked in Kenyan schools. Whether you owed money or were paid up, this always seems to be a moving target.

Then I showed Mama Pamela the clothes, jewelry, and cups I'd brought for the girls at the orphanage. We decided that we would pass them out to them on Thursday or Friday. I wanted to get a lot of good pictures as we passed out these items. Any time the children got anything, they were excited, but especially when it was something new.

I did a lot of reading on my Kindle and a lot of preparing to get back to our school visits in the morning. A lot would happen in the upcoming week, and then a week from tomorrow I would head back to Nairobi and the next evening catch a flight to Paris and start the journey back home.

Monday, June 24, 2013

We left Dago about 9:00 a.m. to visit two schools. We had one student at each. First we went to Koderobara Secondary School to visit Vincent. Duncan and I met with principal, Jean, and the dean of studies. I was able to get both their e-mails so I could keep in touch with them after I left. Jean was clearly very e-mail savvy, especially compared to most Kenyans I had met. He and I talked a lot about the advantages of being able to communicate electronically. I also met with the bursar to understand what money was still owed for the rest of the year. I gave her some Kenyan shillings to get caught up for the moment and told her I would send the rest when I got back home.

We then were able to spend some quality time with Vincent, who was doing very well in school and had done much better in the second term than the first. We went through his report card, encouraging him to do even better, and then we did our picture session and took a video with him. When our visit ended, I was really happy about both our visits there; I'd accomplished everything I wanted to accomplish.

We then made the drive to Oyugi Ogango Girls' Secondary School to visit Isca. This was the most anticipated of my planned visits, and the one that was giving me the most nerves. Isca was a total orphan, having lost both her parents when she was a little baby. She had two older stepbrothers, with whom she did not get along. She was clearly afraid of them, and I had been told they had been physically abusive to her. The only real home Isca had ever known was the Dago Dala Hera Orphanage run by Mama Pamela and Duncan. Although she'd had many issues growing up, she'd gotten the best score on the KCPE of all the girls in her class. Clearly she had great potential. Also, when she was in class eight, she was raped and became pregnant. I was told that an aunt of hers was raising the baby.

In her first year (form one) at the school, her grades were pretty poor. She had several discipline issues, including getting into a fight. She also had several issues getting started in form two, such as getting caught with a cell phone that another girl had somehow sneaked into the school. At that point she was sent home, but she never made it back to Dago because she was afraid of her stepbrothers. I became aware of this, and for about two weeks we had no idea where she was. Eventually Mama Pamela found her and brought her back to school, where she had a long talk with Isca and the staff.

This incident brought up a new issue that was really troublesome for me. When a student like Isca was sent home, she was simply given a little money to get a matatu, and she was gone. It was a long and complicated trip for anyone, but for a teenager it was even more challenging and potentially dangerous.

All of this was settled about six weeks before I arrived on this trip. It was my hope in meeting with Isca today that we could do and say some things that could help her understand what a special opportunity she had with this scholarship and how crucial it was for her to work hard, get great grades, and obey the rules of the school.

We spent some time with the bursar, straightening out what money was owed, and then we met with Martha, the principal. We toured the school and talked about Isca. She told us the best person to talk to was the deputy principal, Phelgona, so we stopped in to meet her.

We ended up having a couple of in-depth conversations with the deputy principal and found that she was very knowledgeable about Isca and all her issues. She knew both of the stepbrothers well and understood that Isca was afraid of them. She said that, as a mother herself, she believed that what Isca needed was the love of a mother. At one point she brought Isca in the room with us, and we talked about her issues and challenges. We were direct and firm with her, but we also tried to show her how much we cared about her and believed in her potential. We told her that we knew she could do great things with her life. The deputy principal, who was also her math teacher, noted that math was her poorest subject, and she scolded her a bit for not coming to her and asking for help. We strongly encouraged Isca to go talk to any of her teachers when she did not understand the material.

I then spent some one-on-one time with Isca, taking some pictures and a video. I reviewed all the issues with her, and again I was firm but tried to emphasize that there were many people who cared about her. I talked about how difficult life was for Kenyan children, especially girls, who did not finish high school. I emphasized that when we awarded the scholarship, we made the point that we reserved the right to take the scholarship away from a student who was not working up to his or her potential. I hoped I was getting through to her.

We then went back and talked some more with the deputy principal. I decided to take a chance with a question that I would not have asked in the United States, but I thought I would try it here. When Isca got into trouble, she called one of her stepbrothers because he was her legal guardian. However, we all knew this guy was a big part of the problem. So I asked the deputy principal, "If something happens with Isca in the future where she needs to make a phone call, could she please call Mama Pamela instead of her stepbrother?" In the United States, of course, school administrators would have to say no to this, because they really would have no choice. They would be required to follow the law and call the legal guardian. To my surprise, however, Phelgona looked at me and said that was a good idea, and Duncan agreed. So Duncan gave her Mama Pamela's cell phone number, and we were all set. I felt confident that this would help Isca in several ways.

Then I had another instance of someone asking me for help. The deputy principal was very nice and complimentary about what I was doing, and she went on to talk about some of the other girls in the school who were having trouble coming up with the school fees. She wondered if there was any way I could be of help. This is just another example of how great the need is in Kenya. Phelgona was very kind and respectful, but of course these kinds of situations are always uncomfortable and leave me struggling for words. I have a really difficult time with things like this, as there are so many children in Kenya who need help, and their situations are so sad. Obviously I wish I could help all of them. In the end I had to tell her I was sorry but I could not help. To be frank, as we headed for the car, I was in tears. No matter how many times I face this kind of situation, it never gets any easier.

When I started this scholarship fund, I vowed that it would not just be about me sending money to Dago to send students to high school. In a way, the money part is easy. I promised myself that I would be involved with these students and actively do whatever

I could to help them be successful. Nothing could have better represented this goal than the time I'd just spent with Isca. I am stealing a line from Chris in the documentary *A Small Act*, but I do not want these children to think I am just giving them money. I want to be giving them *hope* that their lives can be better than the lives they had before high school, and that if they work hard, they can make their dreams come true.

Tomorrow we would have our final two school visits, with two scholarship students at each school. So far I was very happy with how things were turning out, and hoped that after tomorrow I would feel the same way.

Tuesday June 25, 2013

Today started out with some question marks because of the announcement last night that the public school teachers (such as the teachers at Dago Primary School) were going on strike as of midnight. Ever since I arrived in Kenya, I'd been hearing about this issue, but I always thought if there was to be a strike, the date would need to be set about a week or two before it actually happened. Thus I learned another lesson: I couldn't think according to the world I was familiar with, but according to how things worked in Kenya.

This was the seventh such strike since 2007. And while the primary teachers had a separate union from the secondary teachers, I learned that, quite often, the secondary teachers would strike in sympathy with the primary teachers. I had great concerns about how this would affect my plans and goals for the week in my visits with high school students.

During my time in Kenya, I had learned more about teachers' pay and how low it was. Duncan, my host, was a primary teacher for thirty-three years before he retired. His salary for his last year of teaching, the highest salary he ever received, was equivalent to about $250 U.S. per month. This was gross income, and then things like taxes were taken out—and while I am not familiar with the specifics,

I was told taxes represented a much higher percentage of overall income than they did in the United States. As a retired teacher, Duncan got a whopping $100 per month.

So upon waking this morning, I found out that the Dago children had all been sent home because school was closed. I had planned to spend Thursday and Friday there, doing things like taking pictures and getting the names of all the class seven and class eight students. I also wanted to talk to their parents about the scholarship fund and meet with the parents of the seven students we were currently sponsoring. Also, I was not sure how the strike would affect our last two high school visits.

We got into our car and headed for St. Mary Goretty's Dede Girls' Secondary School to visit Lencer and Vivian. We had excellent meetings with each of the staff members and received some e-mail addresses. We then spent some quality time with each of the girls, going over their report cards and talking about how they could do even better. We then took pictures and did a video interview with them. It is always great to hear these students talk about how much they appreciate the scholarship and how they intend to give back when they have built a successful life.

I was sitting and talking with Lencer and Vivian when a man who was on the staff stopped by and asked if I would like him to take some pictures of me and the girls with my camera. I was going to have someone do this anyway, so I said yes. After taking the pictures, he started to walk away, but then he came back and asked if he could take some pictures using his camera. This was the point where I should have realized something was up, but I was so focused on continuing my conversation with the girls that I really did not give it much thought. Thus he took some pictures with his camera and then said thanks and walked away.

About fifteen minutes later—at this point Duncan had joined us—the man returned. He came over and handed me three very nice pictures, one of each girl and one of both girls with me, which he had just printed out. I thought he was giving them to me to be nice, but Duncan explained that he wanted money for them. Apparently this was a way he made a little extra money. His first request was for thirty thousand shillings (about $350). I kind of chuckled and then handed the pictures back to him and said no thanks. He and Duncan began talking a bit in Swahili (negotiating, I assumed), and then Duncan looked at me and said the man would accept three hundred shillings (about $3.50). This was a very small amount of money to me, but I knew it would really help him. So I gave him the three hundred shillings and he seemed very happy. Of course I was really annoyed with his first offer, but I decided to just let that slide. I gave the girls the pictures and realized I had learned another Kenyan lesson.

Having finished our time with Lencer and Vivian, we were on our way to St. Pius Uriri High School to visit with Victor and Nicholus. We did our usual meeting with the staff members, getting some e-mail addresses and checking on any balance we might still owe in school fees. Then we got to the part of sitting down with the boys and talking to them about their report cards and encouraging them to do even better. We were sitting in the bursar's office when Victor and Nicholus walked in, and Victor gave me a rather overwhelming surprise: he ran over and gave me a huge hug. As I've mentioned before, when I first met Victor in 2009, he was so shy that he could hardly even look at me when we were talking. In a project that had already given me so many sensational moments, this one was incredibly special.

I have told the story of how I first met Victor and chose him to be the child I sponsored from my first trip. Watching his journey from that moment through St. Benedict's Primary School for class seven and eight to here at St Pius Uriri had been indescribably rewarding.

I also saw Nicholus, and the three of us went to an area where we could talk, take pictures, and do a video. To each of the children I had visited thus far, I'd given a gift of a spiral notebook and two pens, but this visit included a bit more. Nicholus was sponsored through our program by a friend of mine who was a priest. He and his order supported Nicholus, and they'd given me some special gifts for him. There was a card with a picture of my friend, along with several copies of books he had written explaining the gospel to teenagers. I also gave Nicholus a T-shirt from the school where the priest worked. Nicholus was very excited about the gifts.

Because I did not want Victor to feel left out, I had brought a couple of books for him. I gave him Barack Obama's book *Dreams from My Father*, which I had read on my first trip to Kenya, and the Norman Vincent Peale book *The Power of Positive Thinking*. (I explained to him a bit about who the author was.) And for each boy I also had a spiral notebook and a pencil bag with pencils, pens, erasers, and a ruler.

We all ended up talking for quite some time, and it was just an enjoyable visit. Finally we said good-bye to the boys and headed back to Dago. All in all, it was a magnificent day seeing Lencer, Vivian, Victor, and Nicholus. There were so many times I wondered if all the time I'd invested, money I'd raised, and crazy transportation I'd taken to help the children of Dago was really worth it. This day made it clear that it was all worth it. It was the kind of day I wish I could totally share with my family, friends, and donors, the kind of day where I knew it was all worth it because I could clearly see the tremendous amount of good were doing. I knew we had already dramatically improved the lives of these children and made Dago, the country of Kenya, and the entire world a much better place. These moments and memories will never go away and will never stop being incredible.

Since news of the strike, Duncan and I had been talking about how I could still accomplish the things I wanted with Dago's class seven and eight students. I had not realized it, but Duncan had told the headmaster about our plans for Thursday, and it looked like we could have quite a day. In the morning, all the class seven and eight students and their parents and guardians were supposed to come meet with me. I was hoping that the strike would not keep people from showing up. Then in the afternoon, the parents and guardians of the seven students I had just visited were supposed to come to the school for a meeting. If all of that could happen on Thursday, it would be outstanding.

Tomorrow, Wednesday, I was planning to spend the morning at the orphanage to see the girls and watch the nursery school-day care that was located there until the new building was complete. I had a lot I still wanted to get done this week, and then I could have some time on the weekend to relax, wash clothes, pack, read, and get ready for the journey home. On Monday morning I would take a motorbike to Ranen, and from there I'd get on a bus (I was told it would be a pretty nice bus) for the journey to Nairobi and Wendy's. Then on Tuesday I would get on a plane to head home. Thus far the trip had gone very well, but I did miss my home and my family, plus good American food and a nice shower.

Wednesday, June 26, 2013

With the public school strike still on, I had to change my plans to spend time at Dago Primary School the last few days of the week. This morning I spent some time at the nursery school (what Americans would think of as kindergarten), which was still operating, since it was private and being funded by an American volunteer from North Carolina. I watched as the little children worked on numbers. It was only the second year of the program, but it was already paying big dividends. Before this program began, when students started primary school in class one (at six years old), they had no education at all. The only language they knew was Luo; they did not know any Kiswahili or English. Also, they would not have any of the basics in reading, writing, or math. After the first year of the nursery school program, class one students who had participated in it were way ahead of the students who had not. They came to school already knowing their numbers, their alphabet, some English and Kiswahili, and so on. This would be a great benefit to society, for as the young children got a much better start on their education, we could expect to see that by the time they reached classes seven and eight, they would be far more advanced than the current class seven and eight students.

After this I walked around the school grounds. It was strange to have no students there on a Wednesday. There were a few children hanging around, and I did talk to them to a bit. It was so sad to see these students, who needed so much, deprived of the opportunity to attend school. However I had to remember the fact that we had similar issues in the United States.

Then I did quite a bit of walking around the village of Dago, although I always made sure I knew the direction of Mama Pamela and Duncan's compound so I did not get lost. I also did a lot of reading and began the process of organizing my videos and pictures for my post-trip work. Tomorrow we were supposed to meet with the class seven and eight students and their parents, as well as the parents of the seven scholarship students we had just visited. I was still hoping that the strike would not keep people away.

Friday, June 28, 2013

I had not written anything since Wednesday, and it had been a very interesting two days. When Duncan and I arrived at Dago Primary School around 10:00 a.m. Thursday morning, there were no students or parents. I was dejected, as it looked like the strike was going to kill any chance I had of getting pictures of the class seven and eight students and talking to parents. I needed to remember that a ten o'clock meeting in Kenya could really mean eleven, noon, or even later. Add to that fact the complications of the strike that had started on Tuesday, and it was beginning to look like I would not be able to accomplish much at all during my last two weekdays in Dago.

Around 11:00 a.m., that started to change as people began trickling in. Duncan and I stayed at the school until around 4:00 p.m., as eventually a number of the students and parents came so I could take their pictures and we could talk with them about the scholarship fund. Also, Henry, one of the teachers at the school, came by during the day. He opened up the little building that was the teachers' office and let me see reports on the wall listing the class eight students and their most recent scores on the KCPE pretests. I wrote down all this information, as it would give me a good idea of our best candidates for the next round of scholarships. Also, as an educator, I wanted to compare these numbers with the actual KCPE scores to see how well they functioned as predictors.

As the afternoon went on, we had more and more parents and students show up. Duncan was able to stay with me for a while, but then he had to leave. I stayed until everyone was gone, and that was about 4:00 p.m.

There were forty-two students in class eight and fifty in class seven, and for the two-day period I spent at the school, I was able to meet and get pictures of forty-four of them, almost half. While that was disappointing in the sense that if there had not been a strike, I probably would have gotten all ninety-two, considering what things looked like early Thursday morning, I was pretty happy. The volunteer from North Carolina who did a lot to help out this community would still be in Dago for a few days after I left. Assuming the strike was settled, I was sure she would be able to take the rest of the pictures and e-mail them to me when she got home. If by some chance the strike wasn't over before she left, I would have to ask Edwin or George to get the pictures and e-mail them to me.

Probably the best part of Thursday was the 2:00 p.m. meeting Duncan set up for the parents and guardians of the seven students we had just visited at their high schools. Isca's stepbrother came, and there was one parent for each of the other children. This was a tremendous meeting that brought quite a few tears to my eyes. We talked about how well their children were doing, and the parents could not thank me enough for awarding their children this scholarship. I kept telling them about all the sensational family, friends, students, coworkers, and others who had contributed to the scholarship fund to make it a reality. I was able to take several pictures of them with Duncan, and Duncan took pictures of me with them. These are pictures I will always treasure.

I had so many thoughts going through my head as we talked about the scholarship fund with the students and parents. Most of the parents really only spoke and understood their tribal language, so most of the talking was in Luo, with Duncan translating for me. One of my constant thoughts was about the large number of students in Dago and the relatively small number of scholarships I could offer. Even if was lucky enough to be able to sponsor four more students, which at the moment looked pretty unlikely, that meant thirty-eight students in class eight would not get a scholarship. And that did not count the fact that only about half the students who started in class one made it to class eight. Also, the numbers for the girls were much worse because so many of them dropped out of primary school, usually through no fault of their own. At times like this I get very sad, and the sadness can be overwhelming. In private moments, tears will come to my eyes at these thoughts. I just have to keep reminding myself that I can only do what I can do. To steal more words from Chris in *A Small Act*, "I cannot relieve all of the pain and suffering." This ties in to the story of a poor country like Kenya, where so few students go to high school.

I had been thinking a lot about how I wished the government of Kenya would offer free education for all students, but that was not something I could influence in any way. The challenges in Kenya seemed to be giant obstacles. This was a country where there were very few roads that we would actually call roads, and most people did not even have electricity or plumbing, so the idea of free schools seemed to be more than anyone could even hope for.

I had been told that if the Kenyan government were to create free secondary schools, it would have to build five to six thousand new high schools. As if that were not enough of a challenge, there already was a great shortage of teachers, so where in the world would they find that many more? And of course where would they come up with the money to do all this?

My other big thought these past two days was about how tough the teachers were on their students. Maybe in the United States we had become too concerned about hurting the feelings of our students and putting too much pressure on them. Duncan, who was as nice and mild-mannered a person as you could ever meet, was really, really tough on these class seven and eight students as he told them about the scholarship fund and how it worked. He pushed them not just to get a good score on the KCPE but to be number one. He said this over and over to each child. And as I have written and talked about before, from my observations on this trip and others, I've determined that this is how all the teachers there are with the students. Now, I am very critical of how education is handled in my own country of the United States, but I was not about to start criticizing these Kenyans about how they treat their students, since I really understood very little of the history and culture of their education system, despite this being my third trip here. Still, I could not help but worry that some of the students walked away discouraged, thinking, *Why should I even try? After all, I can never be number one.* In reality, though, I had no idea what they thought as they walked away. And of course Duncan was merely telling them the truth. As of now, the vast majority of these students would not be helped by this scholarship fund. Only a few at the top would benefit from this project. I just had to focus on my goals for this fund and do the best I could to achieve them.

Saturday, June 29, 2013

In the morning I had a shower and then breakfast, and then I did some wash before it was time for church. I sat through the three-hour service with Edwin helping me translate. At the end of the service it was announced that communion would be offered right after church. My first thought was, *This must be for people who have been baptized, and that clearly does not include me.* However a couple of the men who knew me encouraged me to participate.

The women went back inside the church, while the men carried a group of benches over and set them down in a circle just outside the church. They sat down and started the process of washing each other's feet. Henry, a teacher from Dago Primary School and a deacon in this church, came over to show me the passage from the Bible about Jesus washing his disciples' feet. Soon a young man was washing my feet and then drying them. I just sat there for a few minutes, thinking I was done, when one of the other men came up to me and said, "You are not done yet." I said something like "What do you mean?" Well, since I'd had my feet washed, I had to wash one of the other men's feet. I was incredibly nervous but tried hard not to show it as I washed a man's feet and then dried them. After that we all washed our hands.

When all the washing was complete, we went back into the church to join the women, who had been doing the same thing. Then the actual communion ceremony started. Eventually they passed out pieces of bread. I few times I heard them use the word *unleavened*. I was just about to put the bread in my mouth when the man next to me said, "No, not yet." About a minute later, it was time for all of us to eat it. It was a bit like matzah, but more like a cookie texture and not as crunchy. There was really no taste to it.

Next it was time for the wine. They passed around a little metal cup full of brownish liquid. When it came time to drink it, I did, but I was not sure what it was. There was very little taste to it, and I do not think it was any kind of wine. I was just not sure what it was, and did not even ask.

Through much of this ceremony I was thinking, *What an experience for a Jewish guy from the southeast side of Chicago!* It certainly was one that I will never forget and I am sure I will share many times. After church it was time for the two old guys, Duncan and me, to sit around and talk. I say "old" because you did not see many people around who were older than their midforties. You saw some, but not many. We talked until dinner and then talked some more, and then we all watched some TV using their solar power. My third trip to Dago was nearing an end.

Sunday, June 30, 2013

It was a day of relaxing, cleaning, washing, and packing—my last day in Dago for this trip. Time had gone by very fast, but I was anxious to get back home to Chris, my family, and my life. In the evening we

143

had a surprise. The only Odoyo child I had never met, Isaiah, arrived in Dago with his American girlfriend, Erin. Isaiah was the third-oldest of the children, and I knew he had a degree in biochemistry. When he arrived, he looked at me and said something like "Brett, I finally get to meet you." At first I was not even sure who he was, but I quickly put the pieces together. I was able to spend some time talking with him and Erin at dinner.

I took a great picture of Duncan, Mama Pamela, Isaiah, and Erin. Mama Pamela was wearing the Dago Scholarship T-shirt I'd given her, so that was something special. The T-shirt was a replication of a gift some of my own students had given me. It was such a special gift that I decided to have a number of shirts like it made to give to friends, relatives, donors, people in Dago, and so forth. It was red with a black map of Africa on the front and the heads of a male and a female student superimposed in white over the map. It said "The Bernard and Elsie Weiss Dago Scholarship Fund" above the map and "Educating Dago One Student at a Time" below it. On the back there was a quote from Mother Teresa: "Live simply so others may simply live."

Monday, July 1, 2013

I got up early and ate breakfast with Duncan, and then I said my good-byes to everyone. At about 8:30 a.m., the guys on the motorbikes came by to carry George, my luggage, and me the mile to Ranen, where we could catch the bus to Nairobi. At around 9:15, the bus arrived—it was a pretty nice bus—and we were on our way. This was the beginning of my journey home to Naperville. We stopped in the much larger city of Kisii for about half an hour, and then in Nakuru for about fifteen minutes, and of course there were a number of other stops to let people off or on.

As we entered Nairobi about 4:00 p.m. and headed toward downtown, it was clear that rush hour was getting started. I have never seen crazier traffic than what I have experienced in Nairobi.

There are way too many vehicles for the roads they have. Everywhere there are people walking on the sides of the road, people on bicycles and motorbikes and of course all the roundabouts. Thanks to Kenya's British colonial heritage, the roundabouts, or what I call rotaries, are everywhere. Also, there are not many streetlights, but a number of police direct traffic. Most of the roads are pretty good, but some are just awful.

We finally arrived at the Oil Libya Gas Station in downtown Nairobi, and right away I remembered that this was where I was taken to meet Patrick on my first full day in Kenya back in 2009, for my first trip to Dago.

Here George and I met up with James, Wendy's driver, for the trip to Wendy and Martin's house. We switched the luggage, and I said my good-byes to George. Then James began the drive, and it was even crazier. It was not a long distance, but it was close to an hour before we arrived.

I was looking forward to a relaxing night and some dinner. I would stay at Wendy's until I flew to Paris the next night. I would probably have Internet access at her home, and I had a list of things I wanted to get done during the day, like pay bills. I would also get full-swing into the process of wrapping up my diary and organizing my pictures and videos. Of course there would be some e-mails and Facebook too.

Tuesday, July 2, 2013

I spent the day in Nairobi, relaxing, reading, and beginning my wrap-up. I started uploading my videos to my YouTube channel, and in the process I took some time to watch videos of the Chicago Blackhawks in the Stanley Cup finals, which they won. At about 6:00 p.m., James picked me up and drove me to the airport to begin my journey home. The itinerary was Nairobi to Paris to Cincinnati and then Chicago. All in all, it was a good trip; I arrived home only one hour late and with all of my bags. It was fabulous to be home.

However, there are a couple of stories to tell from my layover in Paris. The first one happened when I went to get something to eat. It was a cafeteria-style restaurant, and so I picked up a few things and then got in line to pay. There was a lady in front of me who also happened to be from the United States. When it was time for her to pay, she took out some US currency. The guy behind the counter was very polite and patient with her, explaining over and over that he could not take US currency but she could pay with a credit card or go get some Euros to pay for her food. The lady was getting more and more angry that he would not take her money. She yelled loudly that this was United States currency and he should take it. I was trying to stay out of it, but I was tired and hungry and just wanted to pay for my food and go sit down and eat it.

So eventually I looked at this lady and said something like "Ma'am, you are in a foreign country, and when you are in someone else's country, you have to use their money. Someone from France cannot use Euros to buy things in the United States." She looked at me angrily, used some words toward me that I will not repeat here, and stormed off, leaving her food on the counter. I looked at the guy behind the counter and commended him for how patient and polite he was with her. I apologized to him and assured him that most Americans were not like her.

Here is another great story, also from the Paris airport:

I took a seat near the gate, put my stuff down, and was going to read, but I seemed to be too tired to do anything. I was pretty exhausted, and I was anxious to get home to see my family, take a hot shower, and sleep in my own bed. I started a conversation with the American man sitting next to me. He asked me a lot about my trip, so I started telling him about Kenya and Dago, and he asked more questions. He then pointed to his wife and two daughters, who were seated to his right, and he said that were finishing their vacation in Paris. His oldest daughter was in college and had always dreamed of going to Africa. He asked me if I would talk to her, and of course I said yes.

She came over, all excited to talk and ask questions about Africa.

We talked for quite a while, and she had many great questions. Then she asked me how she could take a trip like mine. We exchanged information, and I told her that when we got back home I would connect her with Shana and Village Volunteers. We said our good-byes and headed back to our respective homes.

I kept my promise and connected her with Shana. That connection led to the start of a great relationship between the two of them, and the next summer, this college girl spent a couple of months in three different places in Kenya. It was a great feeling to be a part of this story. You never know what can come from chatting with someone at the airport. The world can get better in many different ways.

It is still amazing to me that all this happened from a chance meeting at Charles de Gaulle. What were the odds of this happening? I feel as though there was a very special power that wanted us to meet. This is just one of so many incredible stories that have come from my work in Kenya.

Trip Summary

My third trip to Kenya was over, and it was just as special as the first two. I kept learning more and more about the Kenyan culture, and that helped me understand how to successfully run the scholarship fund. There were so many remarkable moments. The Kenyan people never ceased to amaze me with their kindness and hard work.

My trip began with Joshua and his incredible students at Pathfinder Academy. He was doing amazing things, and having also spent some quality time with two other schools, Dago Primary School and Emmanuel's Sirua Aulo Academy, I now had a much better understanding of the education system in Kenya.

Joshua was a bright and impressive man who was a master at marketing and knowing how to run a school. With the addition of his extensive knowledge of and background in agriculture, he was running an exceptional operation. His trips to the United States gave him a number of excellent supporters.

My main goal on this trip was to visit the seven children we were now sponsoring, who attended five different boarding high schools. The visits could not have gone any better, and I got excellent pictures and videos to go with them. In addition, I came away with several staff members' names and some e-mails so I could keep in touch with them. In the later part of my trip, despite the strike, I was able to get a lot of quality time with Dago students, teachers, and parents.

My trip definitely helped me improve the scholarship program, and in that sense alone it was a great success. In addition, making new friends at the Pathfinder Academy and renewing old friendships in Dago was very special for me. Whenever I visit Africa, I never cease to be amazed that I am actually there, and I always have a sense of wonder that this place occupies the same planet I live on. There are times I pinch myself to just make sure it is really happening. And each moment only adds to how fortunate and blessed I feel to have been born and raised and lived my life in the United States. I realize how lucky I am to have the parents, family, and friends I have had. It also adds to my passion about how the small minority of us who have had the chance to have the kind of life I have been blessed to have, have an obligation to help the rest of the world who have not been so blessed.

Trip number three to Kenya was over.

I always thought that my parents were continuously on my back but I was mistaken. They were not on my back, but they were watching my back. Thanks for your support mom and dad.
—"44 Great Thank You Quotes for Parents,"
BrandonGaille.com

2015 Kenya Trip

I will identify bright and vulnerable children from
my village and support them where necessary.
I will help to bring sources of energy and help to
get food to sustain children and parents.
—Julius, scholarship recipient

I am going to review my 2015 trip in a different manner than I did the other three. Since the bulk of my trip was spent visiting our seventeen scholarship students at twelve different high schools, I will focus on these visits. Also, I spent a lot of time meeting with the teachers and administrators at Dago Primary School, as well as the students and parents. I also made a number of home visits, with several goals in mind. In addition, a teacher friend of mine came with me on this trip, and it was great to have some help and another perspective on what we were doing.

During the first couple of days, I had a very interesting moment with my trip partner. She had done a lot of studying of poverty around the world and had some substantive experiences with it from her travels. After we had been in Dago a few days, she looked at me and said, "I knew there were really poor people in the world, but I just did not realize there were people this poor." This is a great example of why you have to get out of your own world and visit places like Dago to really understand what poverty is like. Books, movies, and documentaries all help you be informed, but they can never be anything close to real-life experiences.

On our way to Dago, we made our usual stop in Nakuru to get something to eat. We went into a restaurant I had been in a few times before. Nakuru is in the heart of Maasai country, and I had forgotten about the fact that Maasai people do not like to be photographed. Back during my visit with Emmanuel in 2011, I would ask if it was okay to take pictures. I was always told yes, but I asked first.

Inside the restaurant, we ordered our food and I took a few pictures. As we started to eat, a man came up to us—I later learned he was the owner of the restaurant—and he was clearly not happy. In a very firm manner, he told me that I was not allowed to take pictures in the restaurant. I apologized to him, but it was clear this was not enough. He asked me to hand him my camera.

This was a camera I had bought for this trip. I have never been very good at photography, so in the past I'd always bought very simple cameras. For this trip, however, I decided I wanted to get a much better camera. So I spent a lot of money on this one, and I spent some time before the trip trying to learn all that it could do. The reality is, as I was sitting there with this man asking me for my camera, I still had very little understanding of how it worked.

So I was very nervous, but I carefully handed the camera to him. Frankly, I was not sure I would ever get it back. Edwin was with me, and he and the man talked a bit in Kiswahili, but most of the conversation was between the man and me. He hit some buttons and began looking at the pictures I had just taken. Then he asked me how to delete them. Being very nervous and not being very familiar with the camera, I simply said it was brand-new and I really did not know how to delete a picture. He did not seem to believe me, and that made me much more nervous. He then hit some buttons and said he had deleted the pictures I had taken.

I was still wondering if he was going to give the camera back. He gave me a stern lecture about never taking pictures there unless I had permission. Of course I was being very polite, saying, "Yes sir," every time I could. Just when it seemed he was about take the camera and leave, he handed it to me without saying anything and walked away. By this time I was visibly shaken; I could feel sweat pouring down my back. I was just relieved to have my camera. Later, when we returned to the car, I looked at my camera and saw that while he had deleted some of the pictures I had taken in his restaurant, he had not deleted them all. Anyway, it was an experience I will not forget, especially the next time I am in Nakuru.

High School Visits

Duncan came with me to all the high schools, as he had on my last trip, and he was a big help in getting us in to see the people we needed to see. He also had a much better understanding of the way the schools were run and the proper way to ask for things. His son George would again be our driver and would help with pictures and videos. Of course another key reason I needed them with me was because I had no idea how to get to the schools without them. There were no real addresses or street signs in Kenya, and obviously no GPS that could get me where I wanted to go. I rented a car and gave George a tip for driving (even though he did not want one), because using matatus and motorbikes for these trips would have taken forever, added some elements of danger, and left me totally exhausted. Also, there would have been no way to really know how long it would take to get from one place to another, as this kind of transportation was very unreliable.

I'd laid out the following goals for these visits:

1. Spend quality time with each student and get pictures and videos of him or her.
2. Spend quality time with the key teachers and administrators at the school.
3. Spend part of that quality time going through the students' most recent report cards.
4. Find out about any of the students' unmet needs, such as books, clothes, supplies, or medical attention.

5. Encourage the students to work even harder and do even better than they currently were.
6. Get e-mail addresses for the staff members we met.

A key issue I need to reiterate is that determining exactly how much we owe a school at any given time is like hitting a moving target. It can get very frustrating, but Kenyans seem to be used to that. Expenses come up during the school year that were not anticipated at the beginning of the year. Also, what is covered by school fees can differ from school to school, as each school is totally independent. I always try to take the position that I want to make sure we are providing everything we need for each student in order to give him or her the best opportunity to be successful. Exactly what that means can vary from school to school and student to student. Also, because of the extreme poverty in Kenya, there is no way we can provide everything.

Since the beginning of our scholarship fund, we have always made it clear to the parents and guardians that we expect them to provide for their children's basic needs with things like toiletries. However, some of our students essentially have no parent or guardian, so we need to help out with this. Also, different parents and guardians have more resources than others. Thus this also becomes a moving target, and we just try to do the best we can within our limited resources, recognizing that we can never provide everything.

Also, I should mention that all our schools are for either boys or girls only. It is my understanding that this is true for most of the high schools in Kenya. Also, they are all boarding schools, which once again seems to be true of most high schools in Kenya.

Agoro Sare High School

Roy, one of our first scholarship students, was now in form four, or his fourth year of high school. He had done exceptionally well his first three years. When we arrived at the school, we went to the principal's office. They sent for him, but he was busy with some things, so we had to wait a bit. As Roy approached us, I noticed that he was wearing a blue shirt as opposed to the white shirt all the other boys were wearing, and so I asked Duncan why. He explained that Roy was the "class leader," which seemed to be the equivalent of what we would call the class president. This was a great note on which to start the visit.

In form four, students spent the entire year getting ready for a test they took at the end of the year, the Kenyan Certificate of Secondary Education (KCSE). This was the high school equivalent of the KCPE, which we used as our main determinant for which students we would sponsor. It was my understanding that this exam would determine such things as whether or not you could get into a Kenyan university, the quality of the university you could go to, and how much help in the form of scholarships you could get. Thus for Roy, there were no report cards to review. We did know from his grades the previous year that he needed to improve in English, Kiswahili, and chemistry. Roy had always wanted to be a lawyer, and that was still his big dream.

Roy's mom's name was Mama Irene. I had known her for several years, and she had been a single parent since Roy was little. I call Mama Irene a "helicopter mom," a term we use here in the West. I have not told her I use this term, as I am not sure I could really explain it to her in a way that was proper and left her knowing I was using it as a compliment. Mama Irene is very protective of Roy. A couple of years ago, I received an e-mail from her. My first thought was, *How am I getting an e-mail from a person who lives in a mud hut with no electricity; probably has almost no understanding of computers, e-mail, and the Internet; and has a limited knowledge of English?* I got past that and read the e-mail.

The beginning part of the e-mail was very typical for Mama Irene. She was letting me know of some of her complaints. None of them were about me; they were mostly directed at the school Roy was going to. She was very different from most of the other parents, who tended to be mild-mannered and polite and never seemed to complain about much of anything. I smiled as I read her complaints, knowing this was just Mama Irene wanting the best for her son. She then went on to thank me over and over for the opportunity Roy had been given. Oh, she also explained that she was sending me this message via a friend who had access to electricity and a laptop and taught her how to write an e-mail. She was clearly very determined to get in touch with me. I replied to her, thanking her for the e-mail and the compliments. I also said that I would see what I could do about the "issues" she raised, even though I knew there was probably little if anything I could do about any of them.

We also spent some quality time with the principal and Roy's class teacher. The class teacher was something like a homeroom teacher, who was able to spend extra quality time with a student like Roy but was also one of his subject teachers. We had an outstanding visit, and when we left I was very happy and felt great about Roy's progress and where he was headed.

Awendo Secondary School, Mulo

We had two students at this school: Boss, who was in form one, and Nelson, who was in form two. Boss was doing very well overall but needed to do better in English and physics. It also looked like we needed to work on getting him a new uniform. Nelson was really struggling. He needed to do better in English, Kiswahili, math, chemistry, history, and government and geography. He'd had some health issues, and we discussed them with him and the staff. He also needed to get his eyes checked, and when we returned to Dago, we talked this over with his mom. She assured us she would get this done. It looked like we needed to work on a new uniform for him too.

We spent a lot of time with the deputy principal and the class teacher for each boy. They were very helpful and appreciated our visit, and we exchanged contact information. A great thing about a visit like this one is that after I leave, I am very confident that our students will get some special attention. We strongly encouraged both boys to keep going to their teachers for extra help, which in Kenya they call school coaching.

Itierio Girls High School

We had two students at this school, Eve and Mayerlize. We had a special ceremony for Eve, who was in form one, as she was being sponsored totally by a couple from Delaware in memory of the woman's mother. Her mom grew up very poor in the United States and was not able to go to high school, although many years later she was actually able to get a college degree. We handed Eve a plaque we had made for the ceremony, and we took pictures and a video. She could not keep the plaque at school, so we brought it back to Dago to give to her mom and dad. Eve was number sixty-one out of the one hundred and seventy-two students in her class, which we considered pretty good. She needed to do better in business studies, English, Kiswahili, physics, history, and home science. We reviewed all this information with her mom back in Dago.

The story on this couple from Delaware is a special one. It began a few years ago when we connected on Facebook. I do not really remember the first connection, but I know it had something to do with Kenya, as they have been there a few times. They had donated to the scholarship fund a couple of times, and then one day they contacted me and said they wanted to sponsor a girl all on their own. This was an incredible moment, and the more I thought about it, the more I hoped I could make it happen again.

Mayerlize was also in form one and was forty-second in the class. She needed to do better in English, Kiswahili, physics, religious education, home science, and computer studies. Back in Dago, we reviewed all of this with her mom.

We also spent quality time with the lady who was both girls' class teacher as well as the deputy principal, and we exchanged contact information with her.

Koderobara Secondary School

Vincent, who was in form four, was our student here, but because of a music festival going on at the school all week, the students had been sent home. So we met with him when we returned to Dago, and he brought up an issue that we dealt with from time to time: school fees. He mentioned that he was going to be sent back home the next week because his fees hadn't been paid. This was quite concerning, as it was our understanding that we were all paid up for the year. We had Duncan check on this via his cell phone, and it turned out that Vincent had misunderstood and all was well.

Vincent was number thirty-two out of the eighty-six students in his class, with a C- average. One of the things I always emphasize to my students and others back in the United States is that grading in Kenya is much tougher than it is in the United States. As and Bs are very tough to come by in Kenya, so I know when a student gets one of these grades, he or she really earned it. Vincent needed to do much better in English, Kiswahili, and math, and better in everything else.

He mentioned that there were a number of books he needed but did not have. We put together a list and began working on getting him these books. Also, the uniform he was wearing was in bad shape—he'd had it since form one—and so we started work on getting a new uniform too.

We met with both the principal and Vincent's class teacher, and the principal and I reminisced about the conversation we had during my visit there two years earlier. I've learned that developing real relationships with the staff at these schools is a very important part of a successful program.

Manyatta High School

Michael was our student here, and he was in form one. He was doing very well—number three out of fifty-two students, an A- average. The subjects he needed to do better in were Kiswahili, history, and government. Like Vincent, Michael needed several books, and so we told him we would work on getting them. He also had a uniform issue for us to work on. We spent quality time with both the deputy principal and his class teacher and exchanged contact information with them. Needless to say, I was very happy with Michael's progress.

Moi Nyabohanse Girls' High School

Our student here was Faith, who was in form two. We found that she was really struggling. She had had a lot of health problems but said she was fine now. She had talked to the staff about this, and we were not quite sure what to make of all of it. When we talked to her mom back in Dago, she said that Faith had trouble seeing and that she was going to take her to get her eyes checked. Faith was number thirty-three out of fifty-five, with a D+ average. She needed to do much better in math, English, biology, chemistry, religious studies, and geography. I noticed that her shoes were in terrible shape, so we were going to work on getting her new ones. We also had some book needs that we would work on.

This was the first school visit where we ran into the issue of not really being welcome. I had always felt that we should contact these schools ahead of time to set an appointment, because that is what I would do in my world, but Duncan had assured me that we did not need to do that. And up till now, all our visits had gone fine, but the principal here was clearly not happy with us just showing up. She said we could have some time with Faith, but just a little bit. Eventually Faith's class teacher joined us and was very nice and welcoming, and we got some good quality time with him and Faith.

The bottom line was that Faith needed a lot of help to get on a successful track. I hoped that with all the time we spent with her, her class teacher, and her family back in Dago, we had begun that process. I'll have to admit it was a bit painful getting through this visit; however, I knew in my heart this was a very difficult task I'd taken on. I was a teacher. In my world there were always going to be a lot of bumps in the road. Here in one of the poorest places on earth, there were certainly going to be a lot more.

Ogutu–Migori Secondary School

Ralph was in form two, and he was ranked seventeenth out of sixty-one, for a C average. This gives you an idea of how tough Kenyan teachers are in grading. While his rank was not bad, he was struggling. He needed to do much better in business studies, English, Kiswahili, biology, geography, and religious studies. There were several books he needed, and he also had a uniform issue we needed to work on.

After spending some quality time with Ralph and his deputy principal and class teacher, I emphasized that he needed to go to a lot more consultations, spending extra time with teachers to get help in areas where he was having a tough time. After exchanging contact information with the staff, we were on our way.

Oyugi Ogango Girls' Secondary School

Our student Mackline was in form two here, and there was also Isca, who should have been in form four. You might recall that Isca was our first girl chosen in the program, back in 2012. I shared some of her story when I wrote about my visit two years earlier. She'd had an especially rough childhood, having been raped when she was in class eight (an aunt was raising her baby), and she'd never known her parents, as they died when she was an infant. The only home she knew was the girls' orphanage in Dago. From the time she started high school, she'd had difficulties adjusting. Her social skills were poor, and she constantly had trouble with other girls. Several times she was asked to leave school for a while because of discipline issues. It turned out that she never returned to school for her last year. As of this writing, no one knows where she is.

I've known from the outset that a project like this is not going to be all great successes, but this is still a hard pill to swallow. I do believe that getting in three years of high school will help Isca in many ways. I also hope it will make her very likely to stress the importance of education to any children she has. And I hope that she is well, wherever she is.

Mackline was ranked eighteenth out of seventy-four. She needed to do much better in physics, history and government, math, biology, chemistry, and business studies. She was very shy and reserved, and so it was hard to get her to look directly at us when she was talking. She was a total orphan, meaning that both her parents had passed away. When I was back in Dago, I spent some time talking to her guardian—a member of the school board for Dago Primary School— and he seemed very serious about wanting to help her as much as possible. She was in need of some books, notebooks, shoes, and pens, so we planned to work on that.

We also spent some quality time with the assistant principal and class teacher. (The principal was away at a meeting.) The class teacher seemed very interested in making sure they were doing everything they could to ensure Mackline's success. We were then on our way.

St. Angela Merici Isibania Girls' Secondary School

Beatrice was in form one and happened to be the stepsister of Mama Helda, one of my favorite people in Dago. Her class rank was eighteenth out of seventy-four. Overall she seemed to be having a great first year, but we talked to her about doing better in math, physics, and geography. She was in need of some books, a problem that we needed to work on. She was also in need of some personal items, so we gave her a bit of cash to help her get them.

A cute story came out of the video interview we did with her. When we first started, she was talking very softly and not really looking at us. I gently commented that she did not need to be shy and that I really needed her to look right into the camera. Immediately she looked directly at me, and in a very loud and firm voice, she said, "I am not shy." After that she was a great interview. Her class teacher and principal were great as well. We exchanged information and were on our way.

St. Mary Gorretty's Dede Girls' Secondary School

We were here to meet again with Lencer and Vivian, who by now were in form three. Both girls had had their struggles in the past, but both seem to really be improving. Lencer was number ten out of one hundred, in her class, and Vivian is number forty-four out of one hundred. Lencer needed to do better in English, chemistry, math, and religious studies; Vivian needed to do better in English, Kiswahili, history, and religious studies. Both were also in need of some books. We were able to spend some quality time with Vivian's class teacher and what they called their senior teacher. We also exchanged contact information.

Two years earlier, when I first met with these girls and did the video interview, Lencer was shy and Vivian was outgoing. They both were outgoing on this visit. There is a great story from that interview with Vivian that I have shared with many people. When I asked her what she wanted to be when she grew up, a big smile came to her face. She proudly said, "A broadcast journalist." What is really special about this is that she said this in form one, which meant that a year earlier, when she was in class eight at Dago Primary School and had probably never even seen a television, she never would have given this answer. Now, as a student at a high school that had electricity and television, she clearly had seen a woman reading the news, and somewhere in her brain, she told herself, *That looks like a really great job! I would love to do that someday.* This is just one great example of how getting to a high school—where they have things like electricity, plumbing, television, computers, and Internet—really broadens the world for the children of Dago. The benefit to the child is far greater than any price tag you could put on it.

St. Pius Uriri High School

At St. Pius we were meeting with Victor and Nicholus, who were both in form three. As I mentioned earlier, Victor was really how the whole scholarship program began, when I decided to send him to a private school starting in class seven. Both boys were doing very well.

Victor was ranked number eight out of sixty-three, with a C+ average. Again, this tells you how tough their grading is compared to schools in the United States. Nicholus was number five out of two hundred and eleven, with a B+ average. They were in need of some books, and Nicholus had a uniform issue we needed to address. Both of them could have done better in English and biology. They were getting ready for form four, where they would prepare for the KCSE.

You'll probably recall that Victor was incredibly shy when I first met him in Dago, when he was in class six. I could barely hear him talking, and he would look down at the ground as he spoke. The fact that he'd evolved from the boy who could barely look at me to the one who gave me a big hug in the bursar's office—I already related that story from my last trip—was another sign of the positive impact we were having on the lives of these children and the community of Dago. That moment from two years earlier was still an emotional memory for me.

The staff people we met with were very friendly and seemed very involved in the lives of Victor and Nicholus. Overall I was happy about how positive they were with and about both boys.

Wang' Apala High School

We arrived here to meet with Hillary, who was in form one. He was ranked twenty-ninth out of sixty-six in his class, with a B average. He needed to do better in agriculture and business studies, Kiswahili, math, and geography. Overall he was doing very well. He talked a lot about how great the teachers were at his school. We met with his class teacher and one of his other teachers, who were very helpful, and exchanged contact information with them.

Wrapping up the school visits

This was the last of my visits to the high schools attended by our scholarship recipients. I was very happy with how they had gone, and I felt I had accomplished all the things I'd wanted to get done. Each visit reminded me that in order to make this scholarship program successful, it had to involve much more than just sending money. It was crucial for me to be involved in the students' lives. These visits gave me the opportunity to sit down face-to-face with them, look them in the eyes, and review their progress and what they needed to do better on. I wanted them to know that I cared a great deal for them and was tracking their progress. I wanted them to know that I expected the best from them each and every day. I wanted them to know that I was always there to support them, even though I was eight thousand miles away. I also wanted them to know that I had a connection with the school staff and we were all working together to help them succeed. The value of these visits was far more than any monetary number.

A sad part of my visit was learning that the girls' orphanage in Dago had closed. The previous year's drought had been bad for crops in Kenya; thus the amount of food the orphanage had to feed the girls was inadequate. So the orphan girls were sent home. It was hoped that this year's crops would be better so the orphanage could open back up next year.

Because of this, I made a special point to ask the students at Dago Primary School what food they had eaten that day. Most had not eaten any breakfast and did not expect to have lunch. I was hoping that when they arrived home after school, there would be some food for dinner, but I had no way of knowing for sure. In the past, at least for the orphans, three good meals a day were a given. This is a great example of how a serious drought in Kenya brings about a lot of damage, whereas in my world it may have some negative impact such as higher prices, but the damage is usually very small.

Throughout my visit in 2015, I had meetings with the Dago primary teachers and administrators, and various parents. The scores on the previous year's KCPE exams were lower than those of the year before, and from year to year the Dago scores tended to be much lower than other scores from around the country. I talked with the adults about how we needed to prepare students for this exam so they would get better scores and be better prepared for high school and the years that came after that. I especially talked about the need for the students to do better in English and Kiswahili. In a tiny village like Dago, the "mother tongue" was still the primary language. When the Dago children got to high school, they tended to be behind in other languages, and that deficiency was reflected in their report cards. I noted that when teachers talked to the students, they tended to speak in Luo, when they easily could have spoken in English. I talked a lot about how this change would help the students. This was a big shift from my earlier visits, when I was hesitant to tell the teachers what they should do. Duncan really pushed me to be more forceful with them; he told me all the time that he said the same thing to them a lot, but they tuned him out. He said because I was a teacher from the United States, they would pay much more attention to me.

One of the challenges I had in Kenya was that back in my own country I was very against the trend toward giving more standardized tests; teachers were spending a lot of time "teaching the tests" so the students would get good scores. I felt this was very much hurting education in the United States. Thus I was never totally comfortable pushing teachers and students for better scores on the KCPE and using the results of this test as our main criteria for choosing scholarship recipients. At the end of the day, though, I had to deal with the cards I was dealt and make the best of what we had to keep the focus on helping as many Dago children as possible.

I also spent a lot of my time in Dago making home visits. The main purpose of these visits was to stress the importance of education for all the children in the community. Most of the parents had very little education, and many spoke no or very little English, so Mama Helda would come with me to interpret. Part of what we were fighting was the idea some parents had that *they* did not really get an education and they turned out okay, so their children did not need an education either. Another battle for us was that many parents took the position that their children would never get to high school, so a primary education was really not important. They felt it was better for the children to quit school so they could make money to help the family.

Another big obstacle we faced was the idea among some parents that girls did not need an education. So when I emphasized the importance of education for all children, I always made it a point to mention girls specifically. Some of the parents were not real happy when I said this, but I stayed firm on that point.

I also talked to them about language. I brought up the fact that many of Dago's high school students did not do well in English and Kiswahili. I encouraged them to speak languages other than Luo with their children whenever possible. This was a real challenge for many of the parents, who knew little of English and Kiswahili. Still, I encouraged them to do their best.

Another issue that was very important for me to bring up with them was nursery school. It had been funded and a building built by the volunteer from North Carolina, but her funding was intended to be seed money; the idea was that eventually the community would take over the finances of the school. There were a lot of questions about whether it was going to be able to do this. In each of my home meetings, I stressed the importance of keeping the nursery school open. I talked a lot about how, as a parent and a teacher, I knew the importance of starting education very early. I urged them to do whatever they could to support the school.

As I was doing this, I knew deep inside that I was asking a lot. How could I ask people who were already barely surviving to take some of their very limited resources and use them to support a nursery school for "babies," as they called their five-year-olds, children who would be in school in the United States? I was not sure of the answer to that, but I knew it was crucial that they figure it out. I also knew that in situations like this, there were ways to help other than just giving them money. Parents could volunteer some of their time, and they could donate food to help feed the children.

We also made some home visits to several grandmothers, and these were very sad. These were very elderly women, each with some physical limitations, who were raising several little children. Their children had died (usually of AIDS), and they'd been left to take care of the grandchildren. While all the homes in the village were mud huts, many were fairly well maintained and reasonably clean. These huts were in horrible shape and far from clean. We had very difficult conversations about the challenges they faced, and it was everything I could do to hold back the tears. In one of the poorest communities on the face of the earth, these homes were in far worse shape than most. After several visits I was very shaken.

This brings me to a point I have brought up with many people. In all my visits there were many moments that were tough to deal with. There were a number of times I just went back to my room in Dago and cried for a while, wondering how this could be the same planet I lived on. How could I live in a world where so many people had so much, while these sensational, hard-working, kind people led such difficult lives? At this point I also realized that, for the most part, the people who lived here did not realize just how difficult their lives were, because this world was the only one they knew. I tried to think how I could change all of this, and I realized I could not. However, I could focus on one child at a time, doing the best I could to help that child and then the next. Mother Teresa once said,

If you can't feed a hundred people, then feed just one.

On my last day in Dago, we had a very special few hours with the primary school students, parents, and staff. Chairs and benches were set up in the grass for all of us to sit and talk. It started with me reporting on my two weeks in the Dago area and my time with teachers, parents, and students and my visits to the high schools. With Duncan as my interpreter, I again brought up the importance of doing everything they could to help their children learn languages other than Luo, and of finding ways to keep the nursery school going. I said all this in a very forceful manner, in many ways using the techniques I used for many years selling software. I then stressed the importance of education for all children, especially girls. At one point, in my most direct and firm voice, I said, "I do not want to hear any more of this talk that education is more important for boys!"

When we opened things up to questions from the parents, there were a couple of interesting moments. A man I knew pretty well, who was on the school board, stood up and asked me if I could help pay for him to get solar panels on the roof of his mud hut. While this may surprise you, I got questions like this all the time. He was quite serious. At moments like this one, I put on my economics teacher hat and explain the concept of limited resources. I told him that if I gave him money to put solar panels on his roof, that meant providing fewer children with a high school education. Immediately he said, "No, no, I do not want that." There were a few other questions that were either directly or indirectly asking for money.

Then a man got up and talked in Luo for a long time. The more he talked, the more passionate and angry he seemed to become. He went on and on, and I was thinking, *He must be angry at me about something.* I had to wait for him to finish so Duncan could translate. I was nervous as I waited. Once the man finished, Duncan explained to me that he was yelling at the other parents from Dago. He said that they were always wanting the muzungus to do things for them, and that they must stop asking the muzungus for help and start doing things for themselves. I was relieved once I knew what he'd said, and I thought he'd made a very important point. I knew the resources in Dago were very limited, but I also knew we needed to push people to do as much as they could for themselves. The overwhelming majority of the people there understood that fully.

Toward the end of the meeting, a group of the older students cleared away some chairs and began to sing. They were incredibly entertaining. I then learned about a custom I'd never known about before. As they the students were singing, one of the adults went up to the student who was leading the group and handed him a coin. I picked up on this and handed him a few coins myself.

The very end of the meeting was incredibly special. I had two different women come up to me and hand me a chicken … a live chicken! I quickly handed them over to Duncan, as holding on to a live chicken is not something I have a lot of experience in. Then a man came up to us and gave us six eggs. I was incredibly moved and could not hold back the tears. These fantastic people, who had so little, had given me these two chickens and six eggs as a way of saying thank you. I was thinking, *They may not have dinner tonight because of this*. Their gift was certainly the most special one I had ever received. Of course, for dinner that night, we had chicken and eggs.

Thus my 2015 trip was coming to an end. As always, time went very fast, but I felt that each day we had gotten a lot done. We did take one day off to make a trip to Lake Victoria, about an hour away from Dago, to relax and enjoy ourselves a bit. Victoria is the largest freshwater lake in Africa, and I had never seen it before. While it was very pretty in many ways, it also was just another sign of the poor state of the country. Everything manmade was very plain and simple. Most of the boats were not in good shape, and the buildings were broken-down shacks.

It was time for me to pack up and start the journey home. Once I got back, I would go through my process of putting all the information together and sharing it with all of my donors and potential donors. Each trip I did everything I could to share my journey with others and, I hope, make them feel as much as possible like they were on the trip with me. I would collect my thoughts on each of the children and consider how we could do more to help them. And I would begin again to work on fundraising so we could help as many children as possible in the future.

I wanted to make sure I spent some quality time with my family and appreciated how blessed I was to have all of them. I also wanted to remember how blessed I was every time I turned on the tap, knowing the water was safe to drink. I would think a lot about my late parents, whose names I used for the scholarship fund, and about how blessed I was that they were my parents. Despite growing up very poor, they had worked hard to make sure my brothers and I had the great lives we did.

Security at the Nairobi Airport

On all my trips, of course, I had to go through a lot of security at a lot of airports, and security in Europe was even tougher than it was in the United States. However, neither was any match for the security at Jomo Kenyatta Airport in Nairobi, and when I was coming home in the summer of 2015, security there was the toughest I had ever seen. There were a couple of reasons.

The first was the terrorist group Al Shabaab out of Somalia, which shares part of Kenya's eastern border. Al Shabaab had been growing, and over the previous few years it had conducted several terrorist attacks in Kenya, killing thousands and injuring tens of thousands. One was the terrorist attack at the Westgate Mall in 2013 in Nairobi. The other was the attack at Garissa University in eastern Kenya in 2015.

I knew before I left for Kenya in 2015 that the number of people going there would be down dramatically because of these attacks. The effect was very clear in the airports I went through and in the various places I visited in Kenya. On my other trips, I saw groups of young people from North America, Europe, and other parts of the world, on mission trips. I saw none of that on this trip, and I had heard that basically all religious and other such groups canceled their trips to Kenya for 2015. There were places I would visit in Kenya where normally I would see a lot of Westerners, but now that wasn't the case. There were even several instances when I was boarding a bus and a security guard wanded me and other passengers. To be frank, it did not look like the guards really knew what they were doing, but it was a clear sign of the increase in security by the Kenyan government.

The other reason for the increase in security this trip was that President Obama was going to visit Kenya about a week after I left. It was going to be his first visit as president to his father's home country, and with all the terrorism going on in the world, the Kenyan government began tightening up security very early. So the night we left Nairobi, we had no idea what we were in for. I am glad we got to the airport plenty early, because we needed all the time we allowed ourselves.

While we were still on the road leading into the airport, we had to come to a stop a few miles before the entrance, because there was a long line of cars waiting to clear security. Then at the entrance to the airport grounds, everyone but our driver had to get out of the car and walk through security, where we were wanded by guards. Then we watched as each car was thoroughly inspected and every piece of luggage was opened and inspected. This was just to get inside the airport grounds.

The next level of security was to get into the terminal. All our luggage was scanned, and we were personally patted down. There were people everywhere on this warm evening in Nairobi. It was a very slow and tedious process.

After we stood in line and finally checked in and received our boarding passes, we went through security again—the usual screening of our luggage and being scanned and patted down personally—and then there was one more security check at the gate before we boarded. So by the time we actually got on the airplane, we'd gone through four levels of security, and while there were long lines and a lot of just standing and waiting, I never heard anyone complain. I think everyone realized this amount of security was necessary and made everyone feel safer.

Something else that was on my mind a lot during this trip, as we traveled around Kenya, was how different it was for me to walk there than it was back home. I am not sure why I'd never thought about it before, but as we walked all around Dago and other cities and villages, I began to think about how I could almost always count on navigating a flat surface at home. Whether I was on a road or a sidewalk or in a park, as I took each step I really did not have to worry about a steep step up or down, holes, cracks, and the like. For the most part, I could just walk without worry at home.

Pretty much anyplace I walked in Kenya, however, I could not count on having a flat surface. Whether I was walking on a paved path such as a sidewalk or walking through the grass, I had to carefully watch each step to make sure I would not fall flat on my face. Since I'm not the most coordinated person anyway, I always had to be extra careful in Kenya. This is not a difference I would have thought about before my trips, but it was a significant one. And it is another example of something we Americans take for granted that so many people in the world do not.

So my 2015 trip to Kenya had come to an end.

> Nothing replaces being in the same room, face-
> to-face, breathing the same air and reading and
> feeling each other's micro-expressions.
> —Peter Guber

Some of the Dago Children

Dago Children inside a classroom – 2009

A young Dago girl carrying a baby

Joshua loved my glasses – 2009

Me with a Class 8 Dago Student – 2009

Dago Children – 2009

Three sisters in their mud hut

Two Dago boys – 2009

Children in a Dago Classroom – 2009

Dago Children 2011

Dago girl with baby – 2011

Lencer – 2013

Nicholus – 2013

Roy – 2013

Dago nursery school children - 2013

Me with Nicholus & Victor – 2013

Dago children – 2013

Me with Victor & Nicholus - 2015

Me with Dago Children at School - 2015

Me with Ralph & his teacher – 2015

Me with Beatrice - 2015

Dago Children Flag Ceremony – 2015

Dago Children – 2015

Me and Mackline - 2015

Me with Boss & Nelson - 2015

Me & Michael – 2015

Dago Children with new t-shirts & toothbrushes-2015

The Seven New Scholarship Recipients for 2016

Eunice

Julius

Mercy

Ver 1.21

Moses

Naomi

Phancy

Samwel

Some of the Adults of Dago

The Dago Chief – 2009

Dago woman carrying a bundle

Henry – Teacher at Dago Primary School – 2011

Me with Mama Pamela - 2011

Me with Duncan – 2011

Women's Meeting - Dago Orphanage - 2011

Edwin with son Harun – 2013

Two Dago women – at water pump – 2013

Parents/Guardians of Scholarship Recipients–2013

Parents/Guardians of Scholarship Recipients-2015

Other Pictures

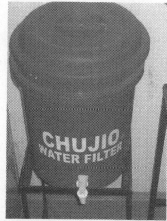

Bartlett the Cow–bought by my students–2011   One of the water filters donated by my students – 2011

Beautiful sunset in Dago – 2011   Scholarship Fund t-shirts – 2013

Entrance to the Dago Dala Here Orphanage

The Dago Church

The Girls Orphanage in Dago

My Room in Dago

The two buildings with rooms for volunteers

A poster at one of the girl's high schools

Buildings

Ranen, Kenya – 2009

Medical Facility near Dago

Inside a Dago Classroom – 2009

My accommodations at Emmanuel's – 2011

Emmanuel's School – 2011

Shopping for school books in Awendo – 2011

My accommodations at Joshua's – 2013

St. Mary Goretty's Dede Girls High School

Sign entering Joshua's Pathfinder Academy – 2013

Agoro Sare High School – 2013

Application Essays

As a part of the application process, we ask our students to write three short essays. On the following three pages are some of the essays students have written.

> I will help parents to know the benefits
> of education for their children.
> I will pay school fees for the orphans so they can study.
> —Roy

B

BENEFITS OF MY EDUCATION TO MY COMMUNITY

Educated community has strong foundation in its people's lives. My education will benefit my community in the following ways:

Curbing poverty: After my education I will be employed. I will get money to assist my family and rais their living standard. This may reduce the rate of poverty in my community.

Financial independent: After being employed or getting self employed, I will depend on myself financially.

Reduces illitracy: My education will help my community to reduce the rate of illitracy in the community.

Community development: Through my education my community will benefit from the developments I will make within the community such as; opening bussinesses, opening learning institutions and being involved in community development projects

B. BENEFITS FROM MY EDUCATION IN THE COMMUNITY

Truly, through my education I would like to set an example to the young growing children. If my education succeed to the high level through my hardworking.

Secondly, In that education I would like to create jobs in the society to reduce theft cases. I would like to supply some shortage of items eg
- Shortage of education funds.
- Basic needs.

I would make my community develop and shine amongst others suppose I succeed in my education. They will bear me witness and also urge pupils to work extra hard even through problems and difficulties.

In my Secondary education I would like to work hard to achieve my goals to serve my community.

The community will escape challenges because they will use what they have at hand. I will build helpful institutions like hospitals, schools and others to serve the community.

I will not be the most essential person but I will create awareness about essential things to have in the communities. Of course, I will be like a sponsor to others, if I succeed in my scholarship.

Truly, they will benefit alot through me.

c

HOW I GREW UP AND THE CHALLENGES I HAVE FACED.

I grew up in a poor family where my parents have no money to take me to school. Sometimes while in school, my fellow pupils do laugh at me because of my raggs and the teachers also send me back home to go and bring the school fees but my parents cannot aford.

My parents have no money to buy food to keep us going and we sometimes go without food. I always look untidy among my fellow pupils because we lack soap to make them clean. I do wash them without soap and wear them while they are still wet.

Education is something very important thing to me. It has made other people's lives shinning. I have been going to school daily and have been noticing the benefits of education day by day.

Education is right, Education is right and Education is life. I have seen other people's life good and meaningfull because education. My parents have given me my right to education. When I complete my Education I'll be able to tell others what education is.

Report Cards

On the next three pages are the report cards of three Dago Scholarship recipients. Their names have been blacked out to protect their identities. Over the years, report cards like these have been an invaluable help as we've tried our best to meet the needs of each student and to understand the unique challenges of education in Kenya.

My family will be happy because they will have a learned
girl who will be able to help them in their daily life.
I shall assist all of the physically disabled
children in achieving their dreams.
—Vivian, scholarship recipient

I will make sure that all orphans and elderly
are fed in our community.
I will give scholarships to all children, both
boys and girls, in our community.
—Isca, scholarship recipient

ST. PIUS URIRI HIGH SCHOOL
P.o Box66 Sare Awendo
Tel: 059-43261
Email:uririhighschool@gmail.com
Website:

END TERM 3 ACADEMIC REPORT-YEAR 2015

NAME: ████████ ADM.NO: 10219 FORM:3 Blue HSE: Pluto

FORM POS: 4 OUT OF 210 CLASS POS: 1 OUT OF 57 MEAN GRADE: B+

T.MARKS: 489 M.MARK: 69.86 T.POINTS: 71.00 M.POINTS: 10.14

SUBJECT	CAT 1	CAT 2	CAT 3	—	PERC%	GRADE	PNTS	POS.	REMARKS	INITIAL
English	46	46	55	—	49	C	6	6	Average	G.M
Kiswahili	56	71	68	—	65	B+	10	1	vizuri	K.E
Mathematics	84	81	78	—	81	A	12	2	Excellent	B.M
Biology	50	49	55	—	51	C+	7	2	Average	N.O
Physics	66	63	59	—	63	B	9	1	Very Good	B.O
Chemistry	74	73	68	—	71	A-	11	1	Excellent	O.E
History & Government	72	85	91	—	83	A	12	2	Excellent	A.E
Agriculture	73	84	73	—	77	A-	11	2	Excellent	O.E

KCPE MARKS	KCPE POS.	KCPE MG.					
358	16	B		489	B+	71	
				700	A	84	

Student's Progress Report

Form 1					Form 2					Form 3					Form 4				
Term	Pos	Out Of	MG	MPTS	Term	Pos	Out Of	MG	MPTS	Term	Pos	Out Of	MG	MPTS	Term	Pos	Out Of	MG	MPTS
1	-	-	-	-	1	9	229	B+	9.36	1	5	-	B+	9.57	1	-	-	-	-
2	-	-	-	-	2	8	230	B+	9.27	2	3	-	B+	10.43	2	-	-	-	-
3	-	-	-	-	3	7	231	B+	9.09	3	4	210	B+	10.14	3	-	-	-	-

Cur. Mean	Prev. Mean	Dev.
10.1429	10.4286	-0.2857

Mean Pnts chart (Form And Term: F1T1, F1T2, F1T3, F2T1, F2T2, F2T3, F3T1, F3T2, F3T3, F4T1, F4T2, F4T3)

Class Teacher's Remarks
Good work but Aim higher for higher grades

* Erastus Oganga*

Head Teacher's Remarks
Good work but Aim higher, you have the potential

Mr. Famuel Okoth Obonyo

Fees arrears Kshs:_____ Next term fees Kshs:_____ Total Kshs_____ Sign_____

School Closed On: 11/19/2015 Next Term Begins On: 5/1/2016

Parent's Sign:_____ Date_____

188

ST ANGELA MERICI ISIBANIA SEC SCHOOL

P.O BOX 21-40414   ISIBANIA
MIGORI, NYANZA 40414-
KENYA
Phone: (+35) 472-9286852 Fax: (***) ***-******

STUDENT'S TERMLY ACADEMIC REPORT   TERM: 1   Year: 2016

Adm no: 584   Name: ████████   KCPE:
Form: 2   stream 2P   Position: 10   Out Of   97

S.No.	Subject	Exam 1	Exam 2	Exam 3	Avg	Comments	Subject Teacher
1	ENGLISH	72	58	0	65 B+	Very good	Mdm. TABITHA
2	KISWAHILI	69	62	0	66 B+	Vizuri sana	Ms. JENIPHER
3	MATHEMATIC	18	20	0	19 E	Work harder	Ms. ESTHER
4	BIOLOGY	70	62	0	66 B+	Good	Mr. CALEB
5	CHEMISTRY	48	48	0	48 C+	Average	
6	PHYSICS	33	50	0	42 C	Improve	Mrs. NYONGESA
7	HISTORY	80	46	0	63 B-	Good	Mr. RIOBA
8	GEOGRAPHY	63	73	0	68 B	Very Good	Ms. JENIPHER
9	CRE	80	85	0	82 A	Excellent	Mdm. SABINA
10	AGRICULTURE	70	85	0	78 A-	Very Good	Mr. CALVINS
11	B/STUDIES	84	64	0	74 B+	Good	Ms. JEROTICH
12		0	0	0	0 ****	***	

Totals: 687   654   0   671   KCSE PROJECTED MEAN:

SUMMARY

Terms Average Mark: 61

Mean Grade: B

Points: 94

graph

Participated actively in: Discipline:

CLASS TEACHER: Mr. MASIAGA
          REMARKS: *Good performance.*

                    CLASS TEACHER'S SIGNATURE: ....

PRINCIPAL: MRS. NYASUBO PRISCILLA
          REMARKS: *Good work , aim higher.*

                    PRINCIPAL'S SIGNATURE: ....

Closing Date 08/04/2016   Next Term Begins On 03/05/2016

                    Next Term's Fee +Arrears: NIL

ITIERIO GIRLS' HIGH SCHOOL,

P.O.Box 2412-40200,KISII. Tel 0735-869662

End Year Report Form 2015

MOTTO: Knowledge is Power

NAME ▮▮▮▮▮▮ Form- 1Y

Term 1-2-3 Year 2015 Adm Number- 2566

SUBJECT	T1	T2	T3	AVR%	S/Rnk	GRD	PTS	REMARKS	Subj Teacher
English	62	72	64	66	34/174	B-	8	Good	Ms.Ntabo J.
Kiswahili	62	45	52	53	108/174	C	6	Wastani	Ms.Ondara G.
Mathematics	58	43	47	49	68/174	C	6	Satisfactory	Mr.Mauti J.
Biology	67	61	56	61	29/174	B	9	Good	Mrs.Jane Z.
Physics	42	24	32	33	141/174	D	3	Poor! Work Hard	Mrs.Mogesa
Chemistry	73	49	56	59	88/174	B-	8	Good	Ms.Azenath
History	48	61	53	54	43/174	C	6	Satisfactory	Mrs.Ogembo A.
Geography	82	32	50	55	66/174	C	6	Satisfactory	Mrs.Ongere G.
CRE	77	73	67	72	31/174	B	9	Good	Mr.Ogega
Home-Science	62	59	56	59	22/76	C	6	Satisfactory	Ms.Masinde
Computer Studies	72	65	59	65	71/174	B-	8	Good	Ms.Mong'eri Venah
Business Studies	34	58	49	47	62/169	C-	5	Satisfactory	Mr.Nyamao M.

Rank This Term: **51 out of 174**

Class Rank: **13 out of 57** KCPE-Marks **279C+**

Total Marks 673 out of 1200

Total Points: 80 out of 144 M-Grade **C+**

Summary of Performance History

Form/Term	F1-T1	F1-T2	F1-T3	F2-T1	F2-T2	F2-T3	F3-T1	F3-T2	F3-T3	F4-T1	F4-T2	F4-T3
TTMks/Perf Index	739	642	641									
Points/M-Grade	92B-	73C	75C									
Overal Rank:	61/171	44/173	48/174									

Class Teacher's Comments

Above average performance. You can do better than this by devoting more time to Physics.

C/Teacher: Ms.Ann Ogembo Sign............. Date:20-11-15

Principal's Comments

Aim higher. You can make these results better next time if you work harder in Physics. Find out why you are not improving on your Mean Grade.

PRINCIPAL
ITIERIO GIRLS' HIGH SCHOOL
P. O. Box 2412-40200 KISII

Principal: Mrs.Stella Matara Sign....... Date:20-11-15

Fee Arrears

KShs Nil

Next Term Fee

KShs 52,100/=

Report Seen by Parent/Guardian.................... Signature.............

Next Term Begins on: 05-01-16

190

Student Letters

Three times a year, I get letters from the scholarship recipients. These letters are very touching and so full of gratitude for the opportunity the students have been given. On the following pages, I've shared three of them.

I will be a role model to the community children so they
can follow in my footsteps in eradication of illiteracy.
I will involve myself fully in projects like building
bridges, making infrastructure and building schools.
—Nicholus, scholarship recipient

I will sponsor needy children like my Good Samaritan does.
I will provide my community with fresh
water so they do not get sick.
—Vincent, scholarship recipient

I want to be a nurse so there will be no sick people
in my community who cannot get help.
I will make sure everyone gets safe water so
no one will suffer from diarrhea.
—Lencer, scholarship recipient

My life has changed since I have joined secondary school and I
am quite proud of it. My life in Koru Girls School has really made
me change to be a girl of good morals and high self-esteem.
—Naomi, scholarship recipient

Dear Brett Kleirs,

Hallow Brett? Recieve alot of greetings from Dago, Kenya and from me more specifically. Since this is my last year in high school I am looking for success and even best wishes from you. I am glad to report to you that I have had ample time to stay in school despite of an incidence which occured and we had to be out of school for two weeks.

Luckily enough, we were able to be back and sit our pre-mock exams and the results shall be out by next term. It is true that this is an opportunity which many have longed for but am blessed in that case. It is only my humble prayer that the Almighty God will help me through and finally come out a better person and a prosperous life.

It is true that nothing comes on a simpler way for life is always a challenging game but all shall go well and end well by November 2016. I congratulate you and send you my heart felt gratitude and congrats to you as the donors for all that you have done and contributed unto my life. Indeed its great.

Recieve a lot of g salutations from my mum and also thanks. Have a ny nice time and enjoy your Easter holiday. Be blessed.

Yours sincerely,

██████████

██████████

DEBE GIRLS' SECONDARY SCHOOL,
P. O BOX 253,
SARE
15. 04. 2014.

THE BOARD OF DIRECTORS,
BENARD AND ELCIE WEUS
SCHOLARSHIP FUND.

REF: APPRECIATION FOR SCHOLARSHIP FUND.

Thank you very much for the scholarship you offered me, since I started form one.

I have been very happy because all the necessary stationery needed by the school I have been provided with from you. You have been paying my school fees promptly giving me easy time for staying in school while other students are sent home for school fees.

Now that you have taken all my responsibility, I shall try by all means to work harder and perform better than how I have been doing.

Again I would like to appriciate our brother whom you left us in his hands to cordinate our studies because he has been helping greatly whenever there is a problem.

Finally may god bless you.

Yours faithfully

193

Moi Nyabohanse Girls
P.O Box 29
Isibania
21st November 2015.

To
THE BOARD OF DIRECTORS
BRETT WEISS SCHOLARSHIP FUND.
C/O BERNARD AND ELSIE
WEISS SCHOLARSHIP FUND.

Receive warm greetings from me. I am grateful to God for seeing us through year 2015 successfully. I hope you are well. As I write this letter once again I want to inform you about my stay in School this term. Let me just assume everything was fine. Second it is about my performance this term we did subject selection giving us eight subject when we sat for the exams I attained position 64 overall and position 14 in class with a cplus grade. I can say I tried to my best but not to my satisfication. Anyway just give me a room for improvement and I am also at work to achieve the possible 'B' and even get the possible 'A's'. Third I will never forget to appreciate you paying my school fees on time. I have never been sent home for fees. for that I appreciate. With the graph it should arise than for the last term graph because last term I get a cplain not a Bplus. Warm greetings from class teacher and My mother God bless you.

Yours faithfully

194

HIV/AIDS Posters from
Kenyan Schools

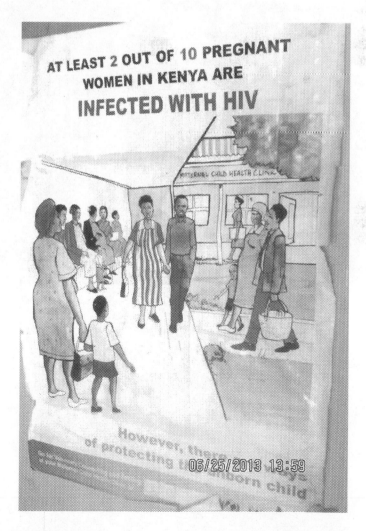

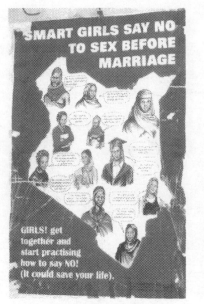 

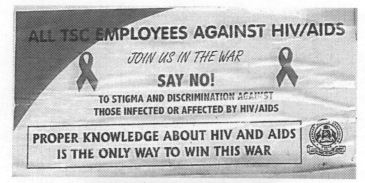

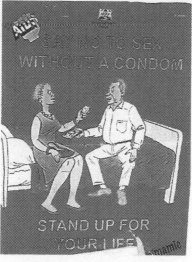

Roy Is Going to a University

In the summer of 2016, we received some of our most exciting news ever about our scholarship fund. Roy, one of our first scholarship recipients, received the results from his KCSE. He'd done very well in high school and exceptionally well on this exam. Out of five hundred twenty-three thousand students in Kenya who took the test, Roy was fifty-fourth. I cannot tell you how excited I was when I heard this news.

Of course it is very exciting that he will get to go to a university. That is exciting news for any child, but especially for a child in Kenya. It is even more exciting for the tiny village of Dago, where so few children over the years have even gone to high school. Here is a boy from this tiny, remote, and incredibly poor village who is now going to attend The University of Nairobi, one of the best universities in Kenya. What a great role model he is for the children of Dago. One of their own is going to get to go to a great university. Yes, *hope*.

Roy always dreamed of being a lawyer, and Irene, his single mom, has had a hard time believing that this dream could come true. I understand that when you live your life in a place like Dago, you begin to think that nothing good can ever happen to you or your family. When I was in Dago in the summer of 2015, Irene asked me if I thought Roy could really be a lawyer. Of course, this was long before we had these test results. I looked at her and said, "Mama Irene, of course he can become a lawyer. He is very smart, gets good marks, and is his class leader." I was very positive with her. As I said that, I was thinking, *I really have no idea*, but there was no need for me to say that to her. Now that Roy has done so well on this exam, it's my hope that he is well on his way to achieving his dream of being a lawyer—and that Irene now believes he can achieve it.

On the next page is a letter Roy wrote thanking the donors of the scholarship fund for their support. I'm including it here because it is so beautifully written and he shows such great appreciation for the support he has been given.

DAGO KOGELLO VILLAGE
P.O. BOX, 21
SARE-AWENDO

3/3/2016

BOARD OF DIRECTORS
THE BERNARD & ELSIE WEISS
SCHOLARSHIP FUND

I want to take this opportunity to write this letter
of gratitude and a lot of thanksgiving to you. It is long
since we communicated but the right time has arrived.

Frankly speaking a new dawn has finally come upon my
life something that was a dream but brought to reality
by your assistance with my high school fees. I lack
the words to express how grateful I am. I am extremely
and sincerely thankful right from the bottom of my heart
for your untold kindness

As we began our journey together in 2012 you promised
to fund my educational needs through my high school
and I was to keep the relationship by working hard
to ensure your assistance was not futile but fruitful.
I thank God for granting me a good grade of A-
in my final examination in high school and without you
I would not be exposed to such situation.

I want to happily report that I was able to score

201

MATHS; A— BIO;A— CHE; B+
HISTORY; A GRE;A— AGRICULTURE;A

My dream of becoming a lawyer is now a
reality and i hope to be a good representative
of the products of your scholarship funds.

As i conclude may the Almighty Lord grant
you with his blessing, for the noble help you
are doing to the unfortunate but bright
students world wide. Thank you

Yours faithfully
Roy.

Stories

Here are some other stories I want to share with you from my time in Kenya and working on this project. It is my hope that they will further your understanding of this journey I have taken, not only in terms of miles, but the learning process I have gone through, and also that you will find these snapshots from my work interesting and useful.

Candy and Chips

I would like to create jobs in the society.
I will work hard to achieve my goals so I can serve my community.
—Samwel, scholarship recipient

Shortly after I started the scholarship program, I started something new with a few of my students in Bartlett, and at first it had nothing to do with Dago. I asked my advanced placement students to do some work that would require them to put in extra hours at school. They had a variety of choices, but in general the work had to be done after school, in the evenings, or on Saturday. To thank them for putting in this extra time, I made a variety of candy, chips, and cold drinks available to them.

It quickly became known among the students in the building that I had candy, chips, and drinks in my classroom, and I started having students—some I knew, and others I didn't—come by to ask if they could have some. I told them the snacks were just for my students who were putting in extra time. Then one day one of these students asked me a question that really threw me a curve and made me think. He asked me if he could have some, saying he would make a donation to the Dago scholarship fund in return. A light bulb went on in my head as I realized I had never thought about this before.

I ended up telling him yes, and I set up a plastic bin for the money. Of course over the next few days, I had other students make the same offer. I then took an old plastic ice cream bin and decorated it with pictures of some of the Dago children. I made a sign saying students could donate money for candy and chips. (I decided not to do it for the drinks, as that would have been a bit much.) I also put up a sign briefly explaining what the scholarship fund was about. I requested donations of seventy-five cents for candy and fifty cents for chips. I decided I would only do this on Fridays. Please note that I was accepting donations for the chips and candy, not selling them.

They became a big hit around school, and of course this gave me a new way to raise money for the scholarship fund. I had to go out and buy the snacks, so it cost me some money, but I set it up so that every penny donated went to the scholarship fund. Being a nonprofit, I was able to buy everything tax-exempt, and I set up an account with a warehouse store near me that always has great prices. Initially I was thinking that this would allow me to raise some additional money, and over the years it certainly has; I average about ninety dollars a week in "revenue." Overall, though, between giving a lot of snacks away to my advanced placement students and giving out freebies other times when I thought it was important, it was costing me a lot more money than I was raising for Dago. But I considered the trade-off worth it, in part because I pretty quickly I learned that there were other benefits in doing this.

Teachers often talk about "teaching moments," and it turned out that accepting these donations created many, many very special teaching moments. I often have students I don't even know come to donate, and I always ask them if they know what the donation is for. I don't want them to think I am just selling candy and chips. When it's their first time donating, they usually have no idea, and so I'll tell them about the children of Dago and what their lives are like. I talk about the education challenges in Kenya and how and why so few children, especially girls, get to high school. This has led to terrific discussions on the topic. It's a real eye-opener for these students when they learn how children in Dago live and how tough life is for them. I always make sure to thank them for helping the children of Dago, Kenya, go to high school.

Many of my most precious teaching moments in recent years have come this way. There were a few times when a small group of students came into my room after the last period on a Friday and ended up sitting with me for over an hour, just asking questions. These questions led to serious and substantive discussions from which they learned a lot—not only about what life is like in Dago but also about how and why I set up the scholarship fund and the logistics of making it work.

All of this, in addition to other ways I get the word out about the scholarship fund, has made Dago very well known around the entire school. This is a very special and unexpected benefit, one I never could have envisioned when I first started.

Never doubt that a small group of thoughtful, committed citizens can change the world; indeed, it's the only thing that ever has.
—Margaret Mead

My Dentist

I will help to make better roads in the
society so traveling will be smooth.
I will build hospitals that are not expensive
because a lack of money can lead to death.
I would like to provide loans to young
women to help them start businesses.
I will make sure that children are immunized for some
common communicable diseases such as polio.
I will make sure there are campaigns for HIV/AIDS
so those who do not know the cause of such diseases
will be educated on how to prevent this disease.
—Eve, scholarship recipient

A few years ago I was visiting a new dentist, and during my appointment I ended up chatting quite a bit with the fabulous young couple who opened the practice. In the course of that conversation, we talked about my work in Kenya. They were very interested and asked many questions. It was another one of those times when it hit me that people were much more interested in this kind of story than I ever would have thought before I made my first trip. Before I left that day, they ended up handing me a very generous check for the scholarship fund. What a wonderful feeling it was to go back home after this great conversation and have more money for the children of Dago.

When I was back at the dentist's office about a month before my trip in 2015, we had another great conversation about Dago. They had a lot more questions, and then they asked me if I would be interested in bringing some toothbrushes to the children there. Of course I said yes. I left that day with a bag of about fifty toothbrushes. I have some great pictures of Mama Helda handing them out to a group of children. She told me this was a valuable donation, as it is hard for families to get toothbrushes because of the cost.

Then during another visit to the dentist, I was asked to bring in a picture of myself with the Dago children for the front the desk, so other dental patients could see it as they checked in and out. I went home, printed out a picture with an explanation of the scholarship fund, and put it in a plastic frame. I then added my nonprofit business card, which had our website and contact information, and took the framed picture to the dentist's office. By my next visit they'd put a plastic container by the picture and a sign asking patients to donate whatever they could. The sign said that at the end of the year the office would match whatever their patients put in.

This is just another story about how kind and generous people have been. It is so touching for me when these kinds of things happen, and to see these two outstanding people find their own way to help the children of Dago.

Remember there's no such thing as a small act of kindness.
Every act creates a ripple with no logical end.
—Scott Adams

The Pen

After finishing my education I would like to be a doctor.
I would like to provide light for education so the community
can know what the profit is of going to school.
—Michael, scholarship recipient

During my first morning in a Dago school in 2009, I was sitting in the back of a room where about forty students in class eight were crowded two or three to a desk. The room was made of mud and brick, with a piece of slate in the front wall, serving as a chalkboard. There was no electricity or plumbing. Light came in from the two open spaces that served as windows (there were no actual windows ... just openings) and from tiny holes in the metal roof.

All the students were taking notes as the teacher was talking, and I noticed that one young man kept shaking his ballpoint pen up and down. It was clear that it was running out of ink, and as he kept shaking it, I saw tears coming from his eyes. Since I always carry a few pens on me, I quietly got up, took a pen out of my pocket, and handed it to him. "This is for you," I said. A huge smile spread across his face. "Thank you," he said. And I went back to my seat and watched him taking notes once again.

At the end of class, he came up to me and tried to give the pen back. I said, "That is okay. You can keep the pen." He tried again, but I persisted, explaining several times that I had several pens and I wanted him to keep this one. He seemed shocked, but he smiled, said thank you, and walked away.

As I started to leave the classroom, the teacher came up to me and thanked me for giving the student the pen. When I asked him why the student began crying when the pen ran out of ink, the teacher explained that it was hard for these children to get pens, and the boy was worried he might never get another one. He was wondering how he would be able to continue going to school.

This was my first full day in Dago, and while I was already going through the culture shock of living in a place with mud huts and no electricity or plumbing, this was a real eye-opener. Something as simple as having a pen to write with, something we just take for granted, was a major issue for the children of Dago. This really put everything in a whole new perspective. On each of my trips after that first one, I always made sure to bring lots of pens and other basic school supplies.

One child, one teacher, one book, one pen can change the world.
—Malala Yousafzai

The Religion Class

I will help the children of my village to
help them achieve their dreams.
I will help develop education in my community.
—Faith, scholarship recipient

So many remarkable stories have become very special parts of this Dago journey. One of my absolute favorites is about a group of children and their teacher from an evening religion class at a church in the western suburbs of Chicago.

After learning about the Dago Scholarship Fund through a newspaper article, this teacher contacted me to ask if I could come by her class one evening to talk to her students about the fund. Of course I enthusiastically said yes. She told me that each Christmas, the class picked one charity that they would raise money for as their Christmas gift. She said they wanted to consider the Dago Scholarship Fund, but she could not guarantee they would choose it. No problem, I told her; even if the fund were not chosen, it would be worthwhile to share the story of the wonderful children of Dago, Kenya, with her students.

So I prepared for the evening with a slideshow that included some of my pictures and videos of the children. When I arrived at the church, I took some time to set up my laptop and projector in the classroom. There were about fifteen children there, all excited to listen. I learned that one child's father had spent some time in Kenya when he was in the military.

So I went through my PowerPoint with the pictures and videos, and I told them what it is like to grow up in Dago, sharing some of the same stories I write about in this book. The children had lots and lots of marvelous questions.

About a week later, the teacher called me to let me know that the children had chosen the Dago Scholarship Fund as their Christmas charity. They also wanted me to come to their class Christmas party.

I arrived to see a fantastic party going on, with lots of fun and great food. All the children had been raising money since my last visit, and they handed me a very generous check. Then they did something else that in many ways was even more special: they gave me handmade Christmas cards for the children in Dago. The cards were beautiful, and the children were so very proud of their work. You could tell they'd put a lot of love and thought into each one.

I was not going back to Kenya the next summer, and so I needed some help getting the cards to the children of Dago. At this time we still had no confidence in the Kenyan mail system; shipping anything to Kenya was both expensive and unreliable. As of this writing, we have made some shipments to Kenya with success, although they were still very expensive. About a month after the Christmas party, through some connections, I found someone from the United States who was going to Dago. I sent her the cards and asked her to take pictures of the children reading them. A few months later, she sent me lots of pictures, and I shared them with the teacher and her students so they could see how their work of love had touched the children in Dago.

The next fall I was invited back to speak to the class, and they once again chose the Dago Scholarship Fund as their Christmas charity. I went and made another presentation, and this time I added the story from my first trip about the student at Dago Primary School whose pen had run out of ink. I was invited again to the class Christmas party, and this time, in addition to a generous donation and Christmas cards, the students gave me a bunch of pens for the children. The story about the boy who did not have a pen, and how appreciative he was when I gave him a one, really made an impression on them, and they wanted to do something about it.

So on my trip back to Kenya the next summer, I was able to present the Dago children with handmade cards and a bunch of pens. I took a lot of pictures of the children holding their new pens and reading their cards, so I could share them with the children back home.

On my last day in Dago, the students presented me with a bunch of cards that they had made, asking me to give them to the children back in the United States. The cards were beautiful. They included lots of quotes from the Bible as well as drawings of their churches, homes, children, and families. I was touched by the children's kindness and told them I would share their gifts as soon as I could with the American children.

A few months later, I was back with the children at the Chicago church. After showing them pictures and videos from my most recent trip, I gave them the cards the Dago children had made for them. These cards were made from notebook paper and drawn with pens of various colors. To protect them, I'd paired the cards back-to-back inside plastic sheet protectors. Every child in the class received one sheet protector holding two cards. The children's excitement was electric, and I took a lot of pictures of them reading and enjoying the cards. There were tears in my eyes as I watched them.

The entire experience with the children and teacher at this church was beyond any adjectives I have been able to come up with to describe it. Yes, there was the donated money, and that is always important. Every penny we raise allows us to help more children. However, these young people in the United States did so much more than just donate money. They took their time to put their love and souls into the cards they made for the Dago children, and they added the special gifts of pens. Then the Dago children returned that loving gesture by making cards for the children back in the United States.

It's likely that these children will never meet each another, but together they have created a very special bond that will forever connect them and I doubt any of them will ever forget. A group of children from the suburbs of Chicago made a very special connection with a group of children in the village of Dago, Kenya, one of the poorest places on the face of the earth. This is a very special blessing.

This is all a great example of how I have learned, as this project has grown, that it is much more than just enabling some Dago children to go to high school. While that is obviously our main purpose and extremely important, it has so many other side benefits, and this is just one of them. The project is about so much more than just raising money. These suburban children learned a lot about what life is like in the tiny village of Dago, and they showed so much love and support for children they had never met and probably never would. And the children of Dago learned that there are other children eight thousand miles away who love them and care for them very much. As the saying goes, that is priceless!

> The greatest gift you can ever give another
> person is your own happiness.
> —Esther Hicks

Bartering

> I want to help the orphans in my community with their education
> to pay their school fees and help with clothes and shelter.
> I will help the children by giving them guidance and counseling.
> —Mackline, scholarship recipient

One of the things I learned in my travels to Kenya is that many of the purchases there are made through bartering. I am going to share a couple of my Kenyan bartering experiences, which gave me an opportunity to learn about the culture, practice my negotiating skills, and use some techniques from my years in software sales.

First Trip, Rift River Valley

On my first full day in Kenya, I woke up at Wendy's home and then went to meet Patrick for the trip to Dago. I had told Patrick that I wanted to find a place to buy some souvenirs I could bring back home as gifts, and so as we were driving, Patrick mentioned that we were going through the Rift River Valley. This was a very pretty area on high ground overlooking a large valley. The road was a bit scary, as it wound through the hills above the valley. Being a two-lane road and not in the best of shape, it made for a few moments when I just kind of closed my eyes. The road was packed with all kinds of vehicles, including cars, trucks, and busses, and there were a variety of animals walking on and across the road.

We reached an area with a lot of little shacks, many of which had signs that said things like "Curio Shop" and were filled with handmade items. Patrick motioned to the driver to pull over and stop so we could check them out. I walked around for quite a bit, and eventually I started talking to the shopkeeper, who was very outgoing and friendly, and we began to tell our stories. It turned out she was a little younger than me and her children were about the same age as mine. She was selling a number of things made out of stone and wood. I began to look around.

I saw something I really liked, and so I held it up and asked her how much it cost. I also reminded myself of the currency conversion, about ninety Kenyan shillings to a US dollar. When I asked her the cost of the item, she took it from me, put it on the table, and said, "Don't worry about that right now. Just pick out something else you are interested in." This is when I began to realize that she had some pretty good sales techniques. After looking around some more, I picked out a second item. I asked her about the cost, and again she took it from my hand and told me not to worry about that now—I should just pick out something else I wanted.

I was not particularly happy with her comment, but I wanted to be polite, so I went along with it and picked out a third item. With all three items lying on the table, I asked her the cost. She gave me the same answer, as expected, so I went along and looked for a fourth item. I picked it out, laid it on the table, and of course got the same answer to my question about the cost. At that point I decided I had to draw a line and say no more until I knew the cost. She realized it was time to just give me a price.

To be frank, I don't remember the exact price she gave me, but I think it came out to about $200. So I started negotiating with her and managed to get the price down a bit, but the whole time I was thinking that I did not want to take advantage of this nice lady. I wanted her to make a nice amount of money to help herself and her family. On the other hand, I did not want to be taken advantage of. Patrick, whom of course I had met only a few hours earlier, was standing about fifteen feet from me, and he could see I was getting nervous about this. He was actually chuckling a bit. I was thinking of just saying okay to her last offer when Patrick walked over and, putting his arm around me, looked at the lady and told her that I was his "Kenyan brother" and therefore should be offered the "Kenyan price."

She thought about it a bit and suddenly dropped the price almost by half. Patrick gave me a pat on the back and I told her it was a deal. So what had been about $200 ended up being less than $100. I paid her the money, and she wrapped up each of the items and put them in a bag. I shook her hand as we said good-bye, and I think we both felt it was a good deal.

Fourth Trip, Nakuru

I have already talked a bit about Nakuru, a big city about midway between Nairobi and Dago. It has a very large marketplace and is a common place for busses, matatus, and other vehicles to take a rest stop. I learned that bus drivers get free meals for stopping there so their passengers can take a break and get something to eat. This was a great marketing idea on the part of the local shop owners. There are a number of markets and restaurants in the area, with a wide assortment of things for purchase. When we stopped there, Edwin told us that after we ate he wanted to take us to a place he thought we would like to buy some souvenirs.

We walked a little way down the road to a spot where a well-dressed man had the usual kinds of things for sale on some wooden crates. Edwin introduced us and he and the man talked a bit, and then the man said, "Come with me." We walked into a small wooden shack and then to a locked door. The man unlocked the door, and when we went inside, we were in the nicest shop I had ever seen in Kenya. He had tables and shelves filled with lots of beautiful items, such as jewelry, artwork, and plates. The room was a bit dark, and what I would call mood music was playing in the background. Clearly this room was meant for people with a bit more money.

I started to look around to see what I might be interested in, and my experience was similar to the one from my first trip. When I put an item on the table, I did not get a price, just encouragement to choose more items. When I had several items on the table, I told the man I needed a price before I would choose anything else. In addition to being well dressed, the man was professional and classy. He asked me where I was from, and when I said Chicago, a big smile came to his face and he mentioned the Chicago Bulls and Michael Jordan.

When he wanted to give me the price, he did something I had seen several other vendors do in Kenya. Instead of saying the number, he took out a piece of paper and wrote it down: thirty thousand Kenyan shillings, or about $333. Again, it takes about ninety Kenyan shillings to equal one US dollar. I thought a lot about my first bartering experience in Kenya. I decided I would just cut to the chase and immediately make my offer half of his. So I said, "Fifteen thousand shillings." He thought about it a bit but did not say anything. Then he wrote his new price: sixteen thousand.

I thought again about that bartering story, and I asked him for the "Kenyan price." There was a bit of smile on his face, and he thought for a moment. I noticed that he never made any quick decisions; he was always thoughtful and deliberate. As someone who'd spent much of his life in sales, I thought he was really good at it. Then he gave me his written response to my asking for the Kenyan price after he'd offered sixteen thousand: seventeen thousand. He smiled again and I chuckled, as of course this was not what I was expecting. He was having fun, playing with me.

We went back and forth a few times and ended up settling at fourteen thousand, a bit less than half of his original offer. I probably could have negotiated a bit more, but I was happy with the price and felt good about it.

We shook hands, and he carefully wrapped each item in newspaper and then put it all in a bag for me. All in all, it was a very enjoyable shopping experience, and I felt I ended up with a good deal. We shook hands again and then I headed back to our car. The shopkeeper was definitely someone I would want to go back to on a future trip.

Where you live should not determine whether
you live, or whether you die.
—Bono

Some Thoughts on Fundraising

> I want to build a hospital for treating the sick and acquire
> police officers to maintain security in the society.
> I will build an orphanage for all of the orphans in our community.
> —Nelson, scholarship recipient

Before I started the Bernard and Elsie Weiss Dago Scholarship Fund, I had done various kinds of fundraising, but nothing on the scale or complexity of what I was about to try. I really had no idea whether I could raise a substantial amount of money. I entered the venture with a lot of confidence, but nothing in my background that said I could have any success.

One of the first things I thought about was the impact my fundraising could have on my relationships with family, friends, colleagues, and so forth. I knew I needed to enter this with the firm conviction that I would never allow it to affect any of those relationships. I could not have negative feelings toward anyone who chose not to donate, and also I could not allow the fact that someone had donated change or improve that relationship. Bottom line: my fundraising, and the emotions that went with it, could not affect anything else in my life.

Now that it has been five years since I started, I feel pretty confident that I have kept my conviction. I have to admit, though, that at times I have been tested. One of the challenges is that I have had many people promise me various kinds of help, from actual money to help raising money, and while some of those people have come through on exactly what they promised, others have not. I have learned to be okay with it either way. I know that the people who did not keep their promise did not have any ill intentions. Offering to help raise money to send children from a tiny village in Kenya to high school is always a good thing. However, after the promise is made, the reality of following through can become difficult. This kind of work is often much more difficult than people think it will be.

In our world of very busy people, most of whom are already pretty generous with their time and money, helping with something like the scholarship fund can easily become a low priority and then just get totally lost. Some people apologize when this happens, and I try my best to reassure them that all is well and I understand. In some cases, I totally lose contact with the people who offered to help, and I think it is because they feel bad and want to avoid me. I hope they know that I would never think less of them just because things didn't work out.

Another issue that's a bit tougher to deal with is when people I know who could easily afford to donate some money choose not to. These are all good people who very well aware of my work in Kenya, and some of them even ask me about it. Many are people I thought would donate, but they haven't. Still, I have never, nor would I ever, let it affect how I think about them. If you are going to embark on a similar venture, I strongly advise you to think about these issues and prepare yourself for them.

Another issue ties into the world of social media. Nowadays we can let the world know our opinions on any matter we want to talk about. I tend to have some very strong opinions on world matters. I have had more than one donor contact me to let me know that he or she would no longer donate to this scholarship fund because of my opinion on a certain issue. Obviously this is very difficult for me. It is hard for me to understand someone who would decide not to help children because of my opinion on an issue, but that is the world we live in. Therefore, I put a great deal of thought into what I say in public, including on social media. Should I let this affect the opinions

I give in public? To be frank, I really do not know the answer to this question. I have to set priorities, and I must admit that as I've put more and more work into the scholarship fund, I've tempered the remarks I make publicly. I hate even having to admit that, but it's true. Thus, this is another issue you need to consider before you start a similar journey.

There are also the incredibly positive stories that come out of this work. One awesome story began with Facebook. Through Facebook I connected with a Delaware couple who had been to Kenya several times and were therefore familiar with the issues I was trying to address. They donated a couple of times to the fund, and via Facebook we began to get to know each other more and more. Then one day they surprised me by saying they wanted to sponsor a girl all on their own, in memory of the woman's mother. This was a scenario I had dreamed of, but now I had an offer. They sent in the money, and then I had a nice plaque made up with a picture of the woman's mother and a quote from her, along with the name of the scholarship recipient. During my 2015 visit to Dago, I held a little ceremony during which I presented the plaque to the girl we had chosen. I took some pictures and videos that I sent to the Delaware couple when I returned. They totally enjoyed seeing them.

A few months later, they contacted me and said they wanted to sponsor a second girl in memory of the man's mother. Wow! This was really exciting. So we made up another plaque for the new award. This experience has given me a lot of fresh ideas for fundraising. I will ask for people who might be interested in sponsoring a child on their own, in addition to the way I have been fundraising.

I had a similar experience when a friend approached me wanting to honor her parents by sponsoring a girl. Her parents were very touched, and we helped yet another Dago child.

When I first started raising money, I was a bit shy about it. Over the years, however, I have become more and more assertive. No matter what I do, I know the goal is to raise as much money as I can so I can help more children. I've begun using a lot more tools like press releases, social media, e-mails, and so forth. I have done presentations to many groups, some who donated money and others who just wanted to learn about the story.

A key decision I made early on was to keep my donors well informed about the progress of our students. I wanted them to see over and over the sensational ways their donations were helping make the world a better place. On a pretty regular basis, I use e-mail to share pictures, letters, report cards, and other such information with my donors. I often get questions back from them, showing me that they are paying attention and like what I am sending. Of course another reason I do this is because I want them to keep giving each year.

One reason I have had success is that I continue to visit the Dago community on a regular basis. I am not just collecting money and sending it to Kenya; I go there in person and meet with each of the students as well as their families and the people of Dago. I have worked hard to become an integral part of that community. I think this personal interaction is a must for a fund like mine to be successful.

I would also suggest to anyone wanting to take on a similar project to keep an open mind. There are so many helpful things I have learned from other people that I never would have thought of. I am constantly trying to pick people's brains to get new ideas for how to raise more money.

And before you try to do something like this, make sure you have visited with people in the areas you want to help and have established a real relationship with them. Make sure too that they are people you can trust. I am eight thousand miles away from Dago, and there are a lot of day-to-day decisions that need to be made, and there's no way I can make them. You need help from people who live in the area where you are working and who know the other people in the community and their history and customs.

Finally, I would say never give up, and try not to get frustrated. There will be many stumbling blocks that get in your way, and you must just keep going. There may be a string of negative things that happen, but just one great thing can easily outweigh all the negative ones. It always seems to me that just when I am getting discouraged, something wonderful and completely unexpected happens. There are a lot of kind, generous, caring people in this great world of ours.

We make a living by what we get, but we
make a life by what we give.
—Winston Churchill

How wonderful it is that nobody need wait a single
moment before starting to improve the world.
—Anne Frank

Personal Reflections

I send lots of thank to all of the donors and other well-wishers
who work tirelessly to see me go through my academics.
—Victor, scholarship recipient

One of the side benefits of the traveling I have been doing to Africa is meeting amazing people from all over the world. These are people who are working hard and doing incredible things to help people like the ones in Dago. It is so inspiring to get a chance to talk to them and learn their stories. It is very interesting to hear how they've taken their personal strengths and leveraged them to help people who are living in absolute poverty. It always motivates me to work even harder at what I do.

I tell people over and over that Kenyans are the nicest, most polite, and hardest-working people I have ever met. Every Kenyan I have met has been incredibly kind and welcoming to me. I always hear things from them like "Welcome to our country" and, "We hope you like Kenya and will come back." These people have virtually nothing in the way of material goods, yet they are always so giving and eager to share whatever they have.

People say to me all the time that I must be able to teach the Kenyans a lot. My reply is that the Kenyans have taught me far more than I have taught them. These people have a sense of community that I feel we have lost in the United States. In places like Dago, everyone knows everyone else and they all try to help and look out for each other. While they do work very hard, I feel they also take the time to enjoy life. And while they have few of the things we consider important, they consider themselves blessed for whatever they do have.

Something I get frustrated with when I am in Kenya, but that really is a magnificent trait of theirs, is the way they consider each moment they can share together in person to be very important. In my world, I am always in a hurry, always trying to figure out how I can get more done each day. In Kenya, however, a very common occurrence is that I am walking along with a Kenyan friend and then we run into someone my friend knows. In my world, I would usually say hi and just keep walking, but Kenyans almost always stop and talk for a few minutes or much longer. Of course, I do the meet and greet, but I am anxious to move on to our next task. They take the time to have a real conversation.

This leads me to another part of my Kenyan experience. I have pushed and pushed myself my entire life to make sure I am always on time, and there are few instances when I have not been. I take real pride in that. But my drive for being on time has been seriously challenged during my travels in Kenya.

For the most part, being on time is just not that important to the Kenyan people. They have other priorities that take precedence. Many of those priorities revolve around trying to stay alive. Therefore, many times I have been ready for something at, say, 9:00 a.m., and at 9:30 or even much later, nothing has happened. That never seems to bother my Kenyan friends. They are very calm about it while I'm going nuts. I've had to learn to just try to relax at these moments. What is the saying—"When in Rome …"? For me, now, it is "When in Kenya …" I still am an on-time nut in my world, but this experience has caused me to think more about priorities and realize that even if I am a bit late to something, the world probably will not come to an end.

Ever since my first trip to Kenya, each time I get water from a tap or turn on the shower, I think about my friends back in Dago. I am incredibly blessed that when I want to use water, I never have to worry about how safe it is. Something as simple as clean water is something that millions of people in our world cannot take for granted.

Another thing I have said countless times since my first trip, to my students and to others, is how incredibly blessed we are in the developed world to live the lives we do. I am just lucky. I happened to be born many years ago to fantastic parents on the southeast side of Chicago who, while having grown up poor themselves, worked hard and made sure their three sons had a great life and could get a good education. I or any one of us could have been born in Dago, or in one of the thousands of other villages in the world like Dago—living in mud huts with no electricity or plumbing, not always sure where our next meal was coming from, wearing hand-me-downs from charities, and receiving little to no education, and what education we did receive would not be very good. Yes, we are just blessed.

I have been asked many times over these last few years if I have any regrets about my work in Kenya. I have a very easy response to that question. My only regret is that I waited so long to begin this journey. I was fifty-eight years old before I made my first trip to Africa. I wish I had made it when I was much younger. Of course, I cannot change my past, but I can share my thoughts on it in retrospect. And I think a lot about how my life might be different if I had made my first trip when I was a younger man.

I also frequently have people say to me, "Why are you helping children so very far away when we have so many children in great need right here in the United States." Of course this is a valid question. In recent years, the childhood poverty level in the United States has increased a lot. I have several responses to that comment. First, my work in Kenya has made me more of a public person than I ever thought I would be. I have learned that in order raise money for these children, I have to put myself out there. While the cause of this scholarship fund is the children of Dago, whether I like it or not, I am the face of the cause.

So I tell people that just because I do things to help people in Kenya, that does not mean I don't also help people in the United States; it's just not something I talk about or make public. That is a very private matter to me. I usually add, "The important thing is just to help a child. If you do not want to help a child in Kenya, then help another child. We have so many children in such great need—just help a child."

I then make another point that I know will be controversial for some: When I look at a map of the world, I don't focus on the various colors of the different countries. Earth was not created with borders; those borders were created by people. I really just see one world. And in my world, every child deserves the opportunity to have a great life and get a great education. Where they happen to have been born is irrelevant to me.

Another common remark I hear is something like "If they want a better life, they just need to work harder." Of course I wish that were actually true. And I recognize that hard work is crucial to success in anything in life. However, as I have pointed out, the people of Dago work incredibly hard each and every day. But for the people of Dago—and I would add for most of the poor people in our world— hard work alone will never get them out of poverty. There are issues that need to be addressed that are largely out of their control. No one would actually choose to live in poverty. These people are not looking for a handout; they're just looking an opportunity to succeed.

As I've mentioned, Kenyans often ask me whether there are poor people in the United States. Part of the reason for the question is they look at all of us as being very wealthy—and compared to them, we are. When I tell them we do have poor people in the United States, they look astonished. Then I have to explain that we have a very different definition of poverty. Most poor people in the United States lead lives that are significantly better than the lives of people in Dago. Poverty means different things in different parts of the world.

In our world we have the saying "What do you get for someone who has everything?" I have changed that phrase around for the people of Kenya: "What do you get for someone who has nothing?" The reality is that whatever I can give to someone in a very poor country is more than what they already have. It could be something as simple as a pencil.

We know that most of the problems in this world stem from a lack of education, which has widespread negative ramifications in a society. For children from a place like Dago, where young people typically don't make it to high school, the odds are heavy that their lives will not be any better than their parents'. In a way, changing that dynamic is pretty simple. With the Dago Scholarship Fund, $3,000 doesn't just give a child a high school education; it also gives that child, and his or her entire community, real *hope* that the future will be better.

Before the scholarship fund, the attitude of many children and parents in a place like Dago was, Why should children work hard in primary school when they know they have no chance to get to high school? This is a big part of why so many children quit school at a young age. They figure they might as well just leave school and try to bring in as much money for their families as they can. Through this scholarship fund, I have seen a great deal of change in that kind of attitude.

I hope that what I have done so far makes my parents up in heaven very proud. None of this could have happened without all the love and guidance I received from them.

Unless you learn to face your own shadows, you will
continue to see them in others, because the world outside
you is only a reflection of the world inside you.
—Unknown

People are sent into our lives to teach us things
that we need to learn about ourselves.
—Mandy Hale

Conclusion

> My community members will benefit from me
> by building hospitals that will get them treatment
> and they will be treated at a fair price.
> I will make sure that the areas where people
> live are clean and free from diseases.
> —Phancy, scholarship recipient

As I sit here at my keyboard, I keep wondering, *How in the world do I write a conclusion to this story of such an important part of my life?* While this book must conclude, this story will never conclude for me as long as I keep waking up each morning. If someone had told me ten years ago that today I would be writing all about my four trips to Kenya and the scholarship fund I started for some children in a remote village there, I would have told them they were crazy. Today the people of Dago are a major part of my life. Some of my best friends are Kenyans. In a way, I have become part of their families and they have become part of mine.

My life has been forever changed because of this marvelous Kenyan journey that started in 2009. For example, the people involved in every aspect of the process—the African friends I have made; all the students, families, and school personnel (from Kenya and my own community); donors; everyone connected to the Bernard and Elsie Weiss Dago Scholarship Fund—have propelled and progressed this incredible work. It is not just about money for high school, it has evolved into bringing *hope* to a people and a country in such great need.

Also, learning how to build a small foundation, including all that is required to develop creative strategies for continuous fundraising, has been eye-opening. This passion and focus requires a deep commitment of time, resources for improvement and growth, sacrifices and choices that must be made, and patience and faith, not to mention flexible planning.

Another bright addition to my life has been the wealth of stories I have gathered along the way, some of which I share here in this book.

So yes, I want to create a world where every child has the opportunity to get a great education. Is that possible? Most people would say probably not. I say, "Of course we can do this. If little old Brett Weiss can send a relatively small group of children to four years of high school for a total of three thousand dollars each, it can be done." When I consider this possibility, I begin thinking things like, *What if one million people in the developed world*—a very small percentage of its entire population—*decided today to ensure that a child from the undeveloped world had an education, at least through high school?* My answer is that the world would immediately be a much better place.

Children in Dago now know that if they work hard, they have a chance to go to high school and beyond. I have seen it change the attitude of their parents and teachers at Dago Primary School. It is amazing what real *hope* can do.

In 2013, the United Nations Educational, Scientific and Cultural Organization published this powerful piece of information:

$16 billion a year in aid would send all children to school in low-income countries. This is about half of the amount Europeans and Americans spend on ice cream annually ($31 billion).

Please know that part of the reason I picked this piece of data is that I am a major lover of ice cream.

We can create a world where every child has the opportunity

to get a great education. But it won't just happen; we have to make it happen. So many of us have the ability to totally change the life of a child, and do it in a way that would have no negative effect on the quality of our own lives. And please remember that this effort requires more than money. It requires ensuring that the money is well spent. It requires ensuring that the children know that in addition to paying their school fees, we really care about them and will take the time to keep up with their progress. It takes having a connection with the staff members at the various schools so they are aware of our support and know we want to see each child be successful. It takes real teamwork between donor, child, parents, and community.

Thank you for becoming a part of my journey. I hope I have given you some new perspectives on our world. I hope I have made you cry and laugh a bit. I hope I have encouraged you to make it a high priority to help every child get the opportunity of a great education.

So do not wait. I ask you to support this mission in whatever way is possible for you. The need is enormous. The smallest token of interest or help can bring about the grandest results. Give *hope*. Go out and help a child today. Go out and make the world a better place. I encourage you to take your own personal journey. I promise you it will dramatically change your life for the better. Is it your time to start this journey? There is no time like the present. Yes, "just give them a hug ... and the rest will be easy."

Asante sana!

We must accept finite disappointment, but never lose infinite hope.
—Martin Luther King Jr.

Hope is being able to see that there is
light despite all of the darkness.
—Desmond Tutu

If you have questions or thoughts, please e-mail me at DagoScholarshipFund@gmail.com.

If you want to know more, or if you want to help us help more students from Dago, Kenya, get a high school education, please visit HopeForDago.org and click on Donate. This takes you to the donation page for our parent organization, Village Volunteers. On the drop-down menu, choose Weiss Scholarship Fund and donate whatever you can. Please share this information with family, friends, and coworkers.

As of this writing, we have awarded twenty-four Dago children full (four-year) high school scholarships. Unfortunately, that means that in the five years we have been doing this, about one hundred and fifty students in class eight did *not* get a scholarship. And that number does not even count the roughly 50 percent of Dago children—the percentage is even higher for girls—who never made it to class eight.

Please consider helping us help the children of Dago, or starting your own journey, today!

Brett Weiss

Twitter: @brettteach
Instagram: dagoscholarshipfund
Facebook: Bernard and Elsie Weiss Scholarship

No one has ever become poor by giving.
—Anne Frank

A collage of the twenty-four Dago Children who have been Scholarship Recipients

Top Row: Beatrice, Boss, Eunice

Second Row: Eve, Faith, Hillary

Third Row: Isca, Julius, Lencer

Fourth Row: Mackline, Mayerlize, Mercy, Mayerlize

Fifth Row: Moses, Naomi, Nelson, Nicholus

Sixth Row: Phancy, Ralph, Roy, Samwel

Seventh Row: Victor, Vincent, Vivian

Here are the twenty-four students to whom we have awarded scholarships as of the writing of this book, along with the high schools they attend or attended:

As of the writing of this book here are the twenty-four students we have awarded scholarships to and the name of the high school they are attending or attended.

2016 Students in The Bernard and Elsie Weiss Dago, Kenya Scholarship Fund And The Schools They Attend (By Year in School)		
Name	Name of School	Year
Naomi	Koru Girls Secondary School	1
Phancy	Kadika Girl's Secondary School	1
Eunice	St. Albert's Girls' High School - Ulanda	1
Mercy	St. Albert's Girls' High School - Ulanda	1
Moses	St. Pius Uriri High School	1
Julius	Awendo Secondary School-Mulo	1
Samwel	Mbita High School	1
Eve	Itierio Girls High School	2
Beatrice	St. Angela Merici Isibania Girls Secondary School	2
Mayerlize	Itierio Girls High School	2
Boss	Awendo Secondary School - Mulo	2
Hillary	Wang'Apala High School	2
Michael	Manyatta High School	2
Mackline	Oyugi Ogango Girls Secondary School	3
Faith	Moi Nyabohanse Girls High School	3
Nelson	Awendo Secondary School-Mulo	3
Ralph	Ogutu-Migori Secondary School	3
Victor	St. Pius Uriri High School	4
Vincent	Koderobara Secondary School	4
Lencer	St. Mary Gorrety's Dede Girls Sec. School	4
Vivian	St. Mary Gorrety's Dede Girls Sec. School	4
Nicholus	St. Pius Uriri High School	4
Previous Award Recipients		
Isca	Oyugi Ogango Girls Secondary School	
Roy	Agoro Sare High School (Awaiting University Placement)	

Sunrise in Dago, Kenya

As we were getting close to printing this book, we announced eight new scholarship recipients, bringing our total number to thirty-two. Here are the names of those eight students:

Girls	Boys
Christine	Donald
Hazel	Brian
Marion	Shalton
Lorren	Maxwel

Come on This Journey and Be Inspired!

As I started to leave the classroom, the teacher came up to me and thanked me for giving the student the pen. When I asked him why the student began crying when the pen ran out of ink, the teacher explained that it was hard for these children to get pens, and the boy was worried he might never get another one. He was wondering how he would be able to continue going to school.

Quote from the book – Brett Weiss

Brett Weiss's book takes an extremely in-depth look at his journey through Dago, Kenya; the various initiatives his foundation started; and the many adverse situations he went through to fulfill his passion of teaching and creating a better community. The story takes you through Brett's life in Kenya and makes you feel right in the middle of all the touching moments he faced. Having Brett Weiss as a teacher in high school, everyone knew his passion for the Bernard and Elsie Weiss Dago Scholarship Fund, but experiencing it through his writing put this all to a refreshing and inspirational perspective. I commend everything that Brett Weiss has done so far and hope everyone can experience the stories he has told in this book.

—Nishu Shah, former student of Brett Weiss,
now a student at the University of Michigan

Reading *Just Give Them a Hug ... and the Rest Will Be Easy* was as if I had arrived in Dago and met the hardworking, sincere people who have become part of Brett Weiss's life now. His personal journals draw you into a world so different from ours it is almost unimaginable, except that Weiss's words share the emotions, the struggles, and the positive outlook of these people so vividly that you are drawn to become part of a solution to provide education to their young students. With his scholarship fund, Weiss has created a path to do that, albeit in one small way. High praise for the work Weiss is doing and for his commitment to education as a way to improve the quality of life in one small community on the other side of the world.

—Jill Holopigian-Rodriquez, retired director of the
Bensenville Community Public Library

Once you start the book, you won't be able to put it down, and perhaps it will inspire you to join Brett in supporting children who desperately want to attend school.

—Shana Greene, executive director,
Village Volunteers

If you want to know more or also help us help additional students from Dago, Kenya, to get a high school education, please go to <u>www.hopefordago.org</u> and click on Donate. This takes you to the donation page of our parent organization, Village Volunteers. On the drop-down menu, choose Weiss Scholarship Fund and donate whatever you can. Please share this information with family, friends, and coworkers. Questions? Email: <u>dagoscholarshipfund@gmail.com</u>

Bernard and Elsie Weiss Scholarship

Open Book Editions
A Berrett-Koehler Partner

Open Book Editions is a joint venture between Berrett-Koehler Publishers and Author Solutions, the market leader in self-publishing. There are many more aspiring authors who share Berrett-Koehler's mission than we can sustainably publish. To serve these authors, Open Book Editions offers a comprehensive self-publishing opportunity.

A Shared Mission

Open Book Editions welcomes authors who share the Berrett-Koehler mission— Creating a World That Works for All. We believe that to truly create a better world, action is needed at all levels—individual, organizational, and societal. At the individual level, our publications help people align their lives with their values and with their aspirations for a better world. At the organizational level, we promote progressive leadership and management practices, socially responsible approaches to business, and humane and effective organizations. At the societal level, we publish content that advances social and economic justice, shared prosperity, sustainability, and new solutions to national and global issues.

Open Book Editions represents a new way to further the BK mission and expand our community. We look forward to helping more authors challenge conventional thinking, introduce new ideas, and foster positive change.

For more information, see the Open Book Editions website:
http://www.iuniverse.com/Packages/OpenBookEditions.aspx

Join the BK Community! See exclusive author videos, join discussion groups, find out about upcoming events, read author blogs, and much more! http://bkcommunity.com/